P9-BIR-133

A Taste Of Italy

FROM PROGRESSO®

CONTENTS

Copyright © MCMLXXXIV by Ogden Foods Corporation.
All rights reserved.
Printed and bound in the United States of America.

Published by Ideals Publishing Corporation.
11315 Watertown Plank Road
Milwaukee, WI 53226
Published simultaneously in Canada.

INTRODUCTION

A Tradition of Home-Cooked Quality

Most of us lead such busy lives today that it's next to impossible to cook as we might like — in those ways that take so much time and effort. And yet, there are still plenty of people who remember and appreciate the delicious rewards of properly prepared food. This, in essence, is what created the opportunity for a company called Progresso.

The story of Progresso began just after the turn of the century in New Orleans when a young immigrant named Vincent Taormina started importing fine quality olive oil, tomato products and other specialties. As the business grew, different family members in other cities joined the organization. In 1928 a merger with Giuseppe Uddo created the Uddo & Taormina Corporation. Though this remained the company title until 1969, its brand name "Progresso," which had been purchased from a New Orleans grocery store for $50 in the 1920s, became much better known to the public.

Through World War II, the Progresso line was still sold mainly in Italian-American grocery stores. But in the postwar era it moved into supermarkets, and the Uddo & Taormina Corporation soon became the largest manufacturer of Italian foods in North America. In 1977, with its brand so familiar to shoppers everywhere, the company changed its name to Progresso Quality Foods.

Putting the word "quality" into the name was more than a casual gesture on the part of Progresso's family-oriented management. Gasper Taormina, the current president, explains, "Quality and flavor are our first priorities and we do whatever we feel must be done to achieve them." Progresso produces over 70 million cans of ready-to-serve soup a year, yet fresh-picked vegetables are still cut by hand, and the soups are still slow-cooked in small batches to give them their homestyle flavor. "I feel," says Mr. Taormina, "that Progresso is living proof that big business need not sacrifice the character and integrity of a small company in order to prosper."

Progresso's 170 products are packed in a large, modern plant in southern New Jersey, at Vineland. Soups, tomatoes, bread crumbs, sauces, beans, vegetables and appetizer products make up the bulk of production. Olive oil and several other imported products also come through Vineland for quality checks before they go into distribution. When juicy-ripe Jersey tomatoes are in season, the Progresso plant operates 'round the clock, turning some 25 million pounds into a variety of tomato specialties. Offshore, a Progresso fleet of clam boats is busy supplying the fresh clams for the company's increasingly popular clam sauces and soups.

The Progresso operation in Vineland is a study in contrasts — at once following the home-cooked standards of its founders yet using the most sophisticated technology of modern food manufacturing. Progresso products that are hand-prepared and slow-cooked in the traditional manner are also extensively sampled by quality control technicians and sent through a series of rigid quality checks. Overall quality is further reviewed by daily "cuttings" (samplings) in which the executive staff (often including the president himself) makes the crucial judgments. As Mr. Taormina says, "We do whatever we have to do to insure our flavor and quality."

A Taste Of Italy

INGREDIENTS

In Italian cooking the essential ingredient is love. Following that, here are some of the many foods which have made Italian cooking so special.

Pasta

The term "pasta," which translated literally means "paste," refers to the many sizes and shapes of macaroni and noodles used in Italian cooking.

Spaghetti is probably used more than any other with sauces; *spaghettini* (thin spaghetti) is usually served with light sauces and seafood sauces (particularly clam); still thinner, *vermicelli* is found often in soups. *Perciatelli* is a bit thicker than spaghetti. Short, tubular shapes such as *ziti*, *rigatoni* and *penne* go well with thick meat sauces. *Cannelloni* and *manicotti* are large pasta squares rolled, stuffed, sauced and baked. Wide, flat pasta *(lasagne)* is served baked in layers. Other pasta shapes include *farfalle* (bow-ties), *rotelle* (spirals) and *conchiglie* (shells). Pre-stuffed pastas include *ravioli* (small filled squares), *tortellini* and *capelletti*. Some pastas, such as *fettuccine* and *lasagne,* include spinach among the ingredients, which accounts for the pasta's green color. Narrow flat egg noodles are called *fettuccine (tagliatelle* is made from the same egg dough but cut ¾ inch wide). Packaged pasta should be cooked in a large amount of boiling salted water. Start checking doneness at about 7 minutes for *spaghettini*; it should be as the Italians like it, *al dente* (to the tooth), having texture and slightly chewy. (Fresh pasta, found increasingly in many supermarkets, will be done in less time.) Drain immediately (it will continue to cook slightly) in a large colander. Do not rinse with cold water. If pasta is not to be mixed immediately with sauce, place it in a large bowl or pot and stir in a spoonful of butter or a little olive oil to prevent sticking. Serve as soon as possible.

Cheeses

Seasoning cheeses, mild-flavored ingredient cheeses and eating cheeses are all passionately important to the Italian cook.

Parmigiano-Reggiano (Parmesan) is the prized grating cheese of Italy. Firm, aged, it has a mellow, slightly salty taste. To retain freshness, store tightly wrapped in several layers of foil.

Romano (Pecorino-Romano) is sharper, more aggressive than Parmesan and is also a firm grating cheese. A lesser known version, *Pecorino-Romano Sardo,* from Sardinia, has stronger, more piquant flavor. *Ricotta* — a fresh, moist, bland unsalted cheese — is comparable to, but not interchangeable with, cottage cheese. It is used as a filling for some pasta dishes *(lasagne, manicotti, cannelloni)* and for cheesecake and pastries. It is quite perishable and should be used within several days. *Mozzarella,* known as the pizza cheese, is also used in baked pasta dishes such as *lasagne.* When heated it has a rubbery, stringy texture. Be careful not to overheat or it can become tough. *Gorgonzola,* Italy's famous blue-veined cheese, is creamy and rich with a sharp spicy taste. An eating cheese, it is excellent with fruit desserts, especially fresh pears. *Fontina,* from the Piedmont section of Italy, is a semisoft cheese used commonly for melting in *fondutas* (fondues). *Bel Paese,* soft and daintily flavored, and *provolone,* firmer, stronger and slightly salty, are primarily eating cheeses.

Seasonings

In Italy it is often easy to tell where a recipe originated by the particular herbs which are called for. Oregano is most used in the South; its milder cousin, marjoram, flavors the dishes of the North, around the Riviera. Basil, a member of the mint family, is used all over Italy and is a particular favorite in the Genoa specialty, *pesto* (a sauce for pasta). Sage, indigenous to the North and Central regions, should not be used in its ground form; use the whole leaf. It is particularly popular with liver. Rosemary is used with lamb and chicken roasts. Fennel seed flavors Italian sweet sausage and sauces for pasta. Bay leaf is found in many meat, poultry and fish stews. The sweet spices, nutmeg and allspice, are used in pasta and meat dishes in the North, as well as in Sicily. Saffron is traditional in *risotto alla Milanese* (a famous rice dish). Parsley, the large, flat-leafed variety called Italian parsley in this country, is often stirred in at the end of the cooking time to give fresh flavor. Onion is the subtle flavorer of many dishes in the north of Italy close to the Swiss border. Garlic is used throughout most of Italy beginning at the Riviera and Genoa, where it is a high note of *pesto* (along with fresh basil). For best flavor when sautéing chopped or minced garlic, allow it to color only to a light brown; a dark brown produces a strong, bitter flavor.

Cooking Oils

Wherever the olive tree grows in Italy — Tuscany, Liguria and throughout the southern regions — olive oil is the preferred cooking oil. In the regions north of Tuscany cooking with butter is more characteristic. However, there are some cooks throughout the country who prefer to use half butter and half oil for sautéing.

Wines

Italy is the world's top wine producer. Its wines can accompany virtually every dish, and can be enjoyed throughout the meal, from aperitif to after-dinner liqueur. Italy's best known fortified wine is *Marsala* — a smooth wine not unlike sherry — used both for cooking and drinking. Either red or white wines can accompany a meal. Some of the most popular white wines are *Soave, Orvieto, Frascati, Pinot Grigio* and *Verdicchio*. Among the reds, *Bardolino, Brunello, Barolo, Valpolicella* and *Chianti* head the list. The general rule has always been to serve red wines with red meats and whites with chicken and fish, but the borders can be crossed. Some poultry dishes, such as Chicken Cacciatore, are often served with red wine, as are certain shellfish dishes. For cooking, dry white vermouth may be used in place of dry white wine; it keeps indefinitely at room temperature.

Fruits

Fresh fruits, available throughout most of Italy, are particularly delicious and a staple on many menus. Most frequently, fruits are eaten whole, often peeled at the table, served with or without cheese. Pears served with a wedge of *gorgonzola* cheese are a summer dessert; in winter Bartlett or Anjou pears poached in red wine are a favorite. Italian peaches are fragrant and juicy. Both apples and peaches can be baked and stuffed with crushed *amaretti* (Italian macaroons). Green figs, cherries, plums, melons, grapes and strawberries are plentiful in summer. They can be marinated in fruit juice, wine or liqueur.

Vegetables

Italians have endless ways of preparing vegetables. Often, a green vegetable such as spinach or escarole will be quickly sautéed with just a bit of garlic in olive oil as a first course. Or a boiled vegetable such as green beans or asparagus will be served at room temperature as a salad. Some vegetables such as broccoli and cauliflower can become part of a pasta dish. Broccoli combined with *penne* (a tubular macaroni), and eggplant baked with *lasagne* are two examples. Other popular vegetables are tomatoes (botanically, these are fruits), zucchini, sweet peppers, *finocchio* (fennel) and peas.

Beans

Beans are particularly popular in the Italian region of Tuscany. There are several types including red kidney beans, *cannellini* (white kidney beans) and *ceci* (chick peas). *Fagioli* (beans) may appear in appetizers, soups (particularly in minestrone, bean and pasta soups), along with rice, with fish, as part of a main course, in salads, or as a side dish.

Sausages

Each region of Italy has its own sausage specialty. *Luganega*, made in the north of Italy, is a fresh mild breakfast sausage. Our pepperoni is an Americanized version of *salsiccia* which comes from Abruzzi region. Fresh sausage from Naples closely resembles what we call "Italian sausage." It's made "sweet" (with fennel) and "hot" (with red pepper). In the Emilia-Romagna region, where *cotechini* (garlic sausages) come from, many cities have individual specialties. What Americans call baloney is based on a sausage produced in Bologna called *mortadella di Bologna*. Modena, "the city of fine sausages," is known for its *zampone* (stuffed pigs feet), traditionally served with lentils on New Year's Eve.

Nuts

Nuts are often used in Italian cooking. *Pignoli* (pine nuts) are an ingredient in Sicilian *caponata* (an eggplant relish served as part of *antipasto*), and used in *pesto* sauce as a thickening agent. Walnuts, too, are used in a special pasta sauce and are occasionally substituted for the more expensive pine nuts in some recipes. Pine nuts, walnuts, almonds, and hazelnuts are frequently used in desserts and cookies.

APPETIZERS & SALADS

Fried Mozzarella
(Mozzarella Fritta)

These are delicious eaten immediately after the cheese has melted.

1 package (8 ounces) mozzarella cheese
3 tablespoons flour
1 egg, lightly beaten
⅓ cup Progresso Italian-style Bread Crumbs
Progresso Olive Oil

Cut the mozzarella cheese into 2½- x ¾- x ½-inch sticks. Dredge each piece of cheese in flour, dip in egg, then coat with bread crumbs. Place on a plate in a single layer. Refrigerate, uncovered, for 1 hour. In a large saucepan heat olive oil, ½ inch deep, to 350° F. Fry mozzarella sticks, a few pieces at a time, until browned on all sides, about 3 minutes. Add more oil as needed. Do not crowd. Remove with tongs. Drain on paper towels. Serve hot with lemon wedges, if desired. Yield: 12 pieces.

Hot Artichoke Cheese Dip
(Passato di Carciofi e Formaggio)

¾ cup Progresso Tuscan Peppers
1 jar (6 ounces) Progresso Marinated Artichoke Hearts
1 can (14 ounces) Progresso Artichoke Hearts
1 package (8 ounces) shredded mozzarella cheese
¼ cup Progresso Grated Parmesan Cheese
⅓ cup mayonnaise
½ teaspoon paprika

Preheat oven to 350° F. Remove stems and seeds from Tuscan peppers; chop (makes ¼ cup) and set aside. Drain liquid from marinated artichoke hearts into the bottom of a shallow 2-quart casserole. Spread liquid to grease bottom of pan. Drain and discard liquid from canned artichoke hearts. Finely chopped marinated and canned artichokes. Place in a medium bowl. Stir in mozzarella and Parmesan cheeses, mayonnaise and reserved chopped Tuscan peppers. Spread in prepared pan. Sprinkle with paprika. Cover and bake until hot, about 15 minutes. Serve with bread sticks or raw vegetables, or spread on crackers. Yield: about 2½ cups.

Antipasto Spaghetti Salad
(Antipasto di Spaghetti in Insalata)

Meat, cheese, vegetables, savory seasonings and pasta. What more could anyone want?

1 package (8 ounces) spaghetti
1 can (19 ounces) Progresso Red Kidney Beans
1 can (19 ounces) Progresso Chick Peas (Ceci)
¼ cup chopped Progresso Olive Salad (Olive Condite)
2 tablespoons chopped parsley
4 ounces sliced boiled ham, cut in strips
4 ounces sliced provolone cheese, cut in strips
4 ounces sliced hard salami, cut in strips
¼ cup Progresso Roasted Peppers in strips
½ cup Garlic Vinaigrette Dressing (page 10)

Cook spaghetti according to package directions; rinse and drain. Place spaghetti in a large serving bowl. Drain and rinse kidney beans and chick peas. Add to spaghetti with olive salad and parsley. Add half of the ham, provolone cheese, hard salami and roasted pepper strips. Pour Garlic Vinaigrette Dressing over all. Toss to coat. Cover and refrigerate until chilled, about 1 hour. Top with remaining ham, cheese, salami and roasted pepper strips. Yield: 6 to 8 portions.

Vegetable Antipasto
(Antipasto di Verdura)

Marvelous colors and textures here. Covered and refrigerated, this antipasto keeps well for several days.

2 cups cauliflower flowerets
1½ cups zucchini in bite-sized cubes
1½ cups eggplant in bite-sized cubes
1 cup carrots thinly sliced on the diagonal
1 cup celery thinly sliced on the diagonal
1 jar (9¾ ounces) Progresso Olive Salad (Olive Condite)
1 jar (6 ounces) Progresso Sweet Fried Peppers
2 tablespoons sugar
¼ teaspoon crushed red pepper
⅔ cup water
⅔ cup Progresso Wine Vinegar
⅔ cup Progresso Olive Oil

In a large saucepan combine cauliflower, zucchini, eggplant, carrots, celery, olive salad and sweet fried peppers. Add sugar, crushed red pepper, water, wine vinegar, and olive oil. Simmer, covered, until cauliflower is barely tender, 4 to 6 minutes, basting occasionally with pan liquid. Uncover and cool to room temperature, occasionally basting and tossing gently. Cover and refrigerate overnight. Drain before serving. Yield: about 7 cups.

Lentil and Parmesan Dip
(Passato di Lenticchie)

1 can (19 ounces) Progresso Lentil Soup
4 tablespoons Progresso Italian-style Bread Crumbs
¼ cup Progresso Grated Parmesan Cheese
1 tablespoon Progresso Wine Vinegar
4 tablespoons finely chopped parsley
2 tablespoons finely minced onion
Raw vegetables for dipping

In a medium saucepan combine lentil soup and bread crumbs. Bring to a boil. Boil and stir for 1 minute. Remove from heat. Stir in Parmesan cheese, wine vinegar, parsley and onion. Serve either warm or at room temperature with cut-up raw vegetables. Yield: 2 cups.

Red Peppers with Capers
(Peperoni con Capperi)

What could be simpler?

1 jar (7 ounces) Progresso Roasted Peppers
1 tablespoon capers

Arrange peppers on a serving platter. Sprinkle with capers. Yield: 4 portions.

Pepper, Mushroom and Artichoke Kebabs
(Spiedini di Verdure)

Fun, easy to put together. And impressive for company.

1 jar (6 ounces) Progresso Marinated Artichoke Hearts
1 jar (3¾ ounces) Progresso Marinated Mushrooms
½ cup Progresso Sweet Fried Peppers

Drain marinated artichokes and mushrooms; combine and reserve marinades. Cut peppers into 1½-inch-wide strips. Wrap a pepper strip around each piece of artichoke; secure with a toothpick. Place a mushroom at the end of each toothpick. Brush peppers and mushrooms with the reserved marinade. Yield: about 12 appetizers.

Garlic Vinaigrette Dressing
(Salsa per Insalata)

¾ cup Progresso Olive Oil
1½ teaspoons Italian seasoning, crushed
1½ teaspoons minced garlic
½ teaspoon salt
⅛ teaspoon ground black pepper
¼ cup Progresso Wine Vinegar

In a container with a tight-fitting lid combine olive oil, Italian seasoning, garlic, salt and black pepper. Let stand 1 hour for flavors to blend. Add wine vinegar; shake well. Serve over salad greens. Refrigerate any remaining salad dressing. Yield: 1 cup.

Chick Pea Salad
(Ceci in Insalata)

Chick peas add the protein necessary to make this a main-dish salad.

⅓ cup Progresso Olive Oil
2 tablespoons lemon juice
½ teaspoon oregano leaves, crushed
½ teaspoon salt
⅛ teaspoon ground black pepper
1 clove garlic, crushed
1 can (19 ounces) Progresso Chick Peas (Ceci)
1½ cups diced ripe tomatoes
¼ cup chopped green pepper

In a large bowl combine olive oil, lemon juice, oregano, salt, black pepper and garlic; mix well. Drain chick peas. Add to bowl with tomatoes and green pepper. Toss gently. Yield: 3 cups.

Green Bean and Pepper Salad
(Insalata di Fagiolini e Peperoni)

1 pound green beans, cut lengthwise in halves
1 jar (7 ounces) Progresso Roasted Peppers
¼ cup chopped fresh parsley
¼ cup thinly sliced scallion (green onion)
¼ teaspoon salt
⅛ teaspoon ground black pepper
4 tablespoons Progresso Olive Oil
2 tablespoons Progresso Wine Vinegar

Cook green beans, covered, in 1 inch boiling water until crisp-tender, 3 to 5 minutes. Lift cover several times as beans cook to let steam escape. Drain beans. Transfer to a large bowl. Thinly slice roasted peppers; add to beans. Sprinkle with parsley, scallion, salt and black pepper. Add olive oil and wine vinegar; mix gently. Serve at room temperature or chilled. Yield: 6 portions.

Eggplant Marinara
(Melanzana alla Marinara)

A Sicilian specialty that's unusual, simply made and delicious.

1 can (7½ ounces) Progresso Eggplant Appetizer (Caponata)
2 tablespoons golden raisins
¼ cup toasted pignoli (pine nuts)
¼ cup chopped Progresso Roasted Peppers

In a small bowl combine eggplant appetizer, raisins, pignoli and roasted peppers. Spoon into a serving bowl. Serve with crackers. Yield: 1½ cups.

Eggplant Marinara, page 10
Prosciutto and Melon Appetizer, page 12
Vegetable Antipasto, page 9
Red Peppers with Capers, page 9
Pepper, Mushroom and Artichoke Kebabs, page 9
Fried Mozzarella, page 8

Stuffed Mushrooms Florentine
(Funghi Imbotite alla Fiorentina)

1 pound medium-sized fresh mushrooms
5 tablespoons Progresso Olive Oil, divided
¼ cup chopped onion
¼ cup Progresso Italian-style Bread Crumbs
1 package (9 ounces) frozen creamed
  spinach, thawed
½ teaspoon salt

Preheat oven to 350° F. Remove stems from mushrooms; set aside. Brush outside of caps with 2 tablespoons of the olive oil; place in a shallow baking pan. Chop enough of the mushroom stems to make ¾ cup. In a medium skillet heat remaining 3 tablespoons olive oil until hot. Add onion and chopped mushroom stems. Sauté for 3 minutes. Stir in bread crumbs, spinach and salt. Spoon into mushroom caps. Bake until hot, about 15 minutes. Yield: about 20 stuffed mushrooms.

Kebabs Italiano
(Spiedini)

1 jar (3¾ ounces) Progresso Marinated
  Mushrooms
4 ounces Genoa salami
4 ounces provolone cheese
1 jar (7 ounces) Progresso Roasted Peppers

Drain mushrooms; reserve marinade and mushrooms separately. Cut Genoa salami and provolone cheese into 16 cubes each. Cut roasted peppers into ½-inch squares. On a sturdy toothpick or small wooden skewer thread a pepper square, a mushroom, a salami cube, a pepper square, a cheese cube and a pepper square. Repeat on 15 more toothpicks. Brush with reserved marinade. Let stand at least 15 minutes. Serve on lettuce leaves, if desired. Yield: 16 kebabs.

Prosciutto and Melon Appetizer
(Prosciutto e Melone)

Prosciutto with cool fruit is sublime.

10 thin wedges peeled cantaloupe or
  honeydew, about 3 inches long
1 ounce thinly sliced prosciutto

Wrap each cantaloupe wedge with a 4-inch piece of prosciutto, tucking edges under melon. Yield: 10 appetizers.

Egg Fritters
(Fritelle Semplice)

4 eggs, lightly beaten
½ cup Progresso Italian-style Bread Crumbs
¼ cup Progresso Grated Parmesan Cheese
⅛ teaspoon ground black pepper
1 cup Progresso Olive Oil

In a bowl combine eggs, bread crumbs, Parmesan cheese and black pepper. In a small skillet heat olive oil until a drop of batter dropped into the oil instantly stiffens and floats to the surface. Add batter by the teaspoonful, a few teaspoons at a time. Fry until golden on all sides, about 2 minutes. Remove with a slotted spoon. Drain on paper towels. Serve hot. Yield: about 4 dozen.

Italian Salad
(Insalata Italiano)

1 can (19 ounces) **Progresso Chick Peas**
   (Ceci)
4 cups mixed salad greens (Bibb, Boston,
   arrugula, radicchio)
1 cup sliced cucumber
½ cup red onion rings
½ cup yellow or sweet red pepper strips
1 jar (6 ounces) **Progresso Marinated
   Artichoke Hearts**
Garlic Vinaigrette Dressing (page 10)

Drain chick peas. Place chick peas in a salad bowl along with salad greens, cucumber, onion, yellow pepper and marinated artichokes. Toss lightly with Garlic Vinaigrette Dressing. Yield: about 6 cups.

Antipasto Salad
(Antipasto in Insalata)

⅓ cup **Progresso Olive Oil**
3 tablespoons **Progresso Wine Vinegar**
½ teaspoon Italian seasoning, crushed
½ teaspoon salt
1/16 teaspoon ground black pepper
1 clove garlic, minced
1 can (19 ounces) **Progresso Chick Peas**
   (Ceci)
   Lettuce leaves
4 ounces sliced provolone cheese, cut
   in ½-inch strips
4 ounces sliced salami, rolled up
1 jar (7 ounces) **Progresso Roasted Peppers**
1 jar (6 ounces) **Progresso Marinated
   Artichoke Hearts**
   Radish roses

In a medium bowl combine olive oil, wine vinegar, Italian seasoning, salt, black pepper, and garlic. Drain chick peas; add to dressing. Mix lightly. Cover and refrigerate at least 2 hours. Just before serving line a 2½-quart serving bowl with lettuce leaves. With a slotted spoon remove chick peas (reserving dressing) and place in the center of the lettuce-lined bowl. Arrange provolone cheese, salami, roasted peppers, artichokes and radishes in any desired pattern around the chick peas. Serve with reserved dressing. Garnish with Tuscan peppers, if desired. Yield: 8 portions.

Bean and Tuna Salad
(Insalata di Tonno e Fagioli)

2 cans (6½ ounces each) **Progresso Light
   Tuna (Tonno)**
¼ cup chopped fresh parsley
2 tablespoons **Progresso Olive Oil**
¼ cup **Progresso Wine Vinegar**
2 cloves garlic, crushed
¼ teaspoon ground black pepper
1 jar (9¾ ounces) **Progresso Olive Salad
   (Olive Condite)**
1 can (19 ounces) **Progresso Cannellini
   (White Kidney Beans)**
1 can (19 ounces) **Progresso Red Kidney
   Beans**

In a large bowl place tuna; break up with a fork. Stir in parsley, olive oil, wine vinegar, garlic and black pepper. Drain olive salad, reserving ¼ cup of the marinade. Add olive salad and the reserved marinade to the tuna mixture. Drain and rinse cannellini and red kidney beans. Carefully stir into tuna mixture. Serve on a bed of lettuce, if desired. Yield: 8 to 10 appetizer portions.

Mushroom Soup Peasant Style
(Zuppa di Funghi alla Contadina)

4 tablespoons Progresso Olive Oil
12 ounces fresh mushrooms, sliced
2 cloves garlic, crushed
3½ cups beef broth
1 can (28 ounces) Progresso Crushed
   Tomatoes
2 finely chopped Progresso Tuscan Peppers
1 teaspoon marjoram leaves, crushed
1 teaspoon oregano leaves, crushed
2 eggs, lightly beaten
½ cup Progresso Grated Parmesan Cheese

In a large saucepot heat olive oil until hot. Add mushrooms and garlic. Sauté for 3 minutes. Stir in beef broth, tomatoes, Tuscan peppers, marjoram and oregano. Bring to a boil. Reduce heat and simmer, covered, for 20 minutes. Remove from heat. Combine eggs and Parmesan cheese. Using a wire whisk, quickly stir into soup. Serve with thick slices of Italian bread, if desired. Yield: about 2 quarts.

Lentil Soup with Two Cheeses
(Minestra di Lenticchie con due Formaggi)

2 cans (19 ounces each) Progresso Lentil
   Soup
¼ cup dry Marsala or sherry
½ teaspoon oregano leaves, crushed
2 tablespoons butter, softened
2 tablespoons Progresso Grated Parmesan
   Cheese
2 tablespoons shredded Swiss cheese
4 slices (½ inch thick) Italian bread, toasted

Preheat oven to 400° F. In a medium saucepan combine lentil soup, Marsala and oregano. Bring to a boil. Remove from heat. Cover to keep warm. In a small bowl blend butter with Parmesan and Swiss cheeses. Spread over toast. Ladle soup into four 14-ounce oven-proof bowls. Top each with a slice of toast. Place on a baking pan. Bake, uncovered, until cheese is melted and lightly browned, 5 to 7 minutes. Yield: about 4½ cups.

Clam Soup Roman Style
(Zuppa di Vongole alla Romana)

3 tablespoons Progresso Olive Oil
1 clove garlic, minced
2 cans (10½ ounces each) Progresso White
   Clam Sauce
1 can (8 ounces) Progresso Tomato Sauce
1 cup water
⅔ cup dry vermouth or white wine
1 teaspoon oregano leaves, crushed
½ teaspoon salt

In a large saucepot heat olive oil until hot. Add garlic. Sauté for 1 minute. Stir in clam sauce, tomato sauce, water, wine, oregano and salt. Bring to a boil. Reduce heat and simmer, uncovered, for 5 minutes. Serve with toasted slices of Italian bread, if desired. Yield: about 1½ quarts.

Tuna Minestrone
(Minestra di Tonno)

1 can (19 ounces) Progresso Minestrone
   Soup
1 jar (15½ ounces) Progresso Marinara
   Spaghetti Sauce
1 cup water
½ teaspoon oregano leaves, crushed
¼ teaspoon salt
⅛ teaspoon ground black pepper
1 clove garlic, crushed
1 can (6½ ounces) Progresso Light Tuna (Tonno)

In a medium saucepan combine minestrone soup, spaghetti sauce, water, oregano, salt, black pepper and garlic. Bring to a boil. Reduce heat and simmer, covered, for 10 minutes. Drain and flake tuna. Add to saucepan. Simmer until hot, about 2 minutes. Serve with toasted garlic bread, if desired. Yield: about 5 cups.

Italian Salad, page 13

Fish Soup with Garlic
(Zuppa di Pesce al Aglio)

2 cans (10½ ounces each) Progresso White
  Clam Sauce
½ cup chopped onion
1½ cups water
1 teaspoon salt
¾ teaspoon thyme leaves, crushed
¾ teaspoon fennel seed
3 strips orange peel (2 inches each)
1 pound fresh fillets or frozen fish fillets,
  partially thawed
2 egg yolks
¼ cup dry vermouth or white wine

Skim 2 tablespoons oil from the top of white clam sauce. Place oil in a medium saucepan. Heat until hot. Add onion; sauté until tender, about 5 minutes. Add water, salt, thyme, fennel and orange peel. Bring to a boil. Reduce heat and simmer, covered, for 15 minutes. Remove orange peel. Stir in remaining clam sauce. Cut fish into 1-inch chunks. Add to saucepan. Simmer, covered, until fish is opaque, about 2 minutes. Carefully remove fish with a slotted spoon; set aside. In a small bowl beat egg yolks with wine. Add about ½ cup of the hot liquid to the yolk mixture, beating constantly with a wire whisk. Add yolk mixture to saucepan; mix well. Simmer, uncovered, until slightly thickened, about 2 minutes. *Do not boil.* Return fish to soup before serving. Garnish with croutons, if desired. Yield: about 5 cups.

Pasta and Chick Pea Soup
(Minestra di Pasta e Ceci)

We served this topped with grated Parmesan cheese. Traditionally the soup is topped with a spoonful of olive oil. Take your pick.

3 tablespoons Progresso Olive Oil
3 cloves garlic, crushed
1 can (28 ounces) Progresso Crushed
  Tomatoes
3½ cups chicken broth
2 cans (19 ounces each) Progresso Chick
  Peas (Ceci)
2 cups ditalini or elbow macaroni
  (uncooked)
½ cup chopped fresh parsley
2 teaspoons basil leaves, crushed
½ cup Progresso Grated Parmesan Cheese

In a large saucepot heat olive oil until hot. Add garlic. Sauté for 1 minute. Stir in tomatoes, chicken broth, chick peas and ditalini. Bring to a boil. Reduce heat and simmer, covered, until ditalini is cooked, about 15 minutes, stirring occasionally. Stir in parsley and basil. Simmer 2 minutes longer. Serve with Parmesan cheese. Yield: about 2½ quarts.

Spinach and Meatball Soup
(Polpette e Spinaci in Brodo)

1 pound ground beef
1 cup Progresso Italian-style Bread Crumbs
¾ cup Progresso Grated Parmesan Cheese
2 eggs, lightly beaten
½ cup water
7 cups chicken broth
1 cup finely chopped onion
1 cup finely chopped carrots
1 package (10 ounces) frozen chopped
  spinach or 1 head (1 pound) escarole,
  chopped
1 teaspoon oregano leaves, crushed
  (optional)

In a bowl combine beef, bread crumbs, Parmesan cheese, eggs and water. Shape into 1-inch balls; set aside. In a large saucepot combine chicken broth, onion and carrots. Bring to a boil. Reduce heat and simmer, covered, for 10 minutes. Stir in spinach and oregano. Return to a boil. Add meatballs. Reduce heat and simmer, covered, until meatballs are cooked, about 10 minutes. Serve with additional Parmesan cheese, if desired. Yield: about 2½ quarts.

Tuscan Minestrone
(Minestrone alla Toscana)

3 tablespoons Progresso Olive Oil
1 cup chopped onion
1 cup thinly sliced carrots
1 can (28 ounces) Progresso Crushed
  Tomatoes
3½ cups beef broth
⅓ cup regular cooking rice (uncooked)
1 can (19 ounces) Progresso Cannellini
  (White Kidney Beans)
4 cups shredded green cabbage

In a large saucepot heat olive oil until hot. Add onion and carrots; sauté until tender, about 5 minutes. Stir in tomatoes, beef broth and rice. Bring to a boil. Reduce heat and simmer, covered, for 20 minutes, stirring occasionally. Drain cannellini. Add cannellini and cabbage to saucepot. Return mixture to a boil. Reduce heat and simmer, covered, until cabbage and rice are just tender, about 10 minutes. Serve over thick slices of bread and sprinkle with Parmesan cheese, if desired. Yield: about 2½ quarts.

Chicken Broth with Eggs
(Stracciatelle con Pomodori)

6 cups chicken broth
1 can (8 ounces) Progresso Tomato Sauce
2 teaspoons grated lemon peel
⅛ teaspoon ground black pepper
2 cups chopped fresh spinach or 1 package
  (10 ounces) frozen chopped spinach
2 eggs, lightly beaten
⅓ cup Progresso Grated Parmesan Cheese

In a large saucepan combine chicken broth, tomato sauce, lemon peel and black pepper. Bring to a boil. Add spinach. Reduce heat and simmer, covered, for 3 minutes. Using a wire whisk, quickly stir in eggs and Parmesan cheese. Serve with more Parmesan cheese, if desired. Yield: about 2 quarts.

Herbed Chicken and Lentil Soup
(Minestra ai Tre Piatti)

1 can (19 ounces) Progresso Lentil Soup
1 jar (15½ ounces) Progresso Plain Spaghetti
  Sauce
2 cups chicken broth or water
½ cup small-sized pasta (uncooked)
½ teaspoon basil leaves, crushed
1 cup diced cooked chicken

In a medium saucepan combine lentil soup, spaghetti sauce, chicken broth, pasta and basil. Bring to a boil. Reduce heat and simmer, covered, until pasta is tender, about 5 minutes. Add chicken. Heat until hot. Add more broth if a thinner soup is desired. Yield: about 5 cups.

Tuscan Bean Soup
(Minestra di Fagioli alla Toscana)

6 slices (½ inch thick) Italian bread
1 can (19 ounces) Progresso Red Kidney
  Beans
1 can (19 ounces) Progresso Macaroni and
  Bean Soup
2½ cups chicken broth
  About 4 teaspoons Progresso Olive Oil
  Freshly ground black pepper

Preheat oven to 400° F. Cut each slice of bread into thirds. Place on a baking pan. Bake until dry, about 5 minutes; set aside. Drain red kidney beans. In a large saucepan combine kidney beans, macaroni and bean soup and chicken broth. Bring to a boil. Reduce heat and simmer, covered, for 10 minutes. Place bread in the bottom of a soup tureen or individual serving bowls. Ladle soup over bread. Cover and let stand for 5 minutes. Stir gently. Serve with olive oil and black pepper. Yield: about 6 cups.

Rice and Bean Soup
(Minestra di Riso e Fagioli)

2 tablespoons Progresso Olive Oil
2 ounces prosciutto ham, finely chopped
1 cup finely chopped celery
½ cup chopped onion
1 can (28 ounces) Progresso Crushed
   Tomatoes
2 cups water
⅓ cup regular cooking rice (uncooked)
¼ teaspoon ground black pepper
1 can (19 ounces) Progresso Cannellini
   (White Kidney Beans), undrained
1 can (19 ounces) Progresso Red Kidney
   Beans, undrained
¼ cup chopped fresh parsley

In a large heavy saucepot heat olive oil until hot. Add prosciutto, celery and onion. Cook and stir for 3 minutes. Stir in tomatoes, water, rice and black pepper. Bring to a boil. Reduce heat and simmer, covered, until rice is cooked, about 20 minutes, stirring occasionally. Add cannellini, red kidney beans and parsley. Return to a boil. Reduce heat and simmer, covered, for 5 minutes. Serve with Italian bread, if desired. Yield: about 2½ quarts.

Chick Pea Soup
(Minestra di Ceci)

The bread slices will rise to the top as in French onion soup.

2 tablespoons Progresso Olive Oil
1 cup chopped onion
2 cans (19 ounces each) Progresso Chick
   Peas (Ceci), undrained
3½ cups beef broth
1 can (15 ounces) Progresso Tomato Sauce
1 package (10 ounces) frozen chopped
   spinach or 2 cups chopped Swiss chard
1 teaspoon sage leaves, crushed
1/16 teaspoon ground black pepper
8 slices (½ inch thick) Italian bread
¾ cup Progresso Grated Parmesan Cheese,
   divided

Preheat oven to 450° F. In a large saucepot heat olive oil until hot. Add onion. Sauté for 2 minutes. Place contents of 1 can of the chick peas in the container of an electric blender. Cover and whirl until smooth. Add to sautéed onion along with remaining chick peas. Stir in beef broth, tomato sauce, spinach, sage and black pepper. Bring to a boil. Reduce heat and simmer, covered, for 10 minutes. Arrange bread slices in the bottom of a 4-quart oven-proof casserole. Top with ¼ cup of the Parmesan cheese. Ladle soup over all. Sprinkle with remaining ½ cup Parmesan cheese. Bake until cheese is lightly browned, about 8 minutes. Yield: about 2½ quarts.

Bread Soup Florentine Style
(Zuppa di Pane alla Fiorentina)

3 tablespoons Progresso Olive Oil
1 cup chopped onion
1 cup chopped carrots
1 can (28 ounces) Progresso Crushed
   Tomatoes
5 cups chicken broth
1 can (19 ounces) Progresso Cannellini
   (White Kidney Beans), undrained
4 cups broccoli flowerets
2 teaspoons basil leaves, crushed
¼ teaspoon ground black pepper
8 slices (½ inch thick) Italian bread
   About ½ cup Progresso Grated Parmesan
   Cheese

In a large saucepot heat olive oil until hot. Add onion and carrots. Sauté for 3 minutes. Stir in tomatoes, chicken broth, cannellini, broccoli, basil and black pepper. Bring to a boil. Reduce heat and simmer, covered, for 20 minutes. Place Italian bread in a large soup tureen or individual soup bowls. Add soup. Cover and let stand for 5 minutes. Serve with Parmesan cheese. Yield: about 3 quarts.

Rice and Bean Soup
Chick Pea Soup

Veal Cutlets Parmesan
(Vitello alla Parmigiana)

1 pound boneless veal leg, ¼ inch thick (scallopine) or chicken breasts, boned, skinned and halved
2 eggs, lightly beaten
1 cup Progresso Italian-style Bread Crumbs
6 tablespoons Progresso Grated Parmesan Cheese, divided
6 tablespoons Progresso Olive Oil, divided
1 can (8 ounces) Progresso Tomato Sauce
8 ounces mozzarella cheese, sliced

Pound veal between 2 pieces of wax paper with a meat mallet or cleaver until ⅛ inch thick. Dip veal in eggs, then in bread crumbs mixed with 4 tablespoons of the Parmesan cheese. Press crumb mixture into meat. Place scallopine on a platter. Refrigerate for 30 minutes or freeze for 5 minutes. In a large skillet heat 3 tablespoons of the olive oil until hot. Add a few pieces of the veal. Brown about 2 minutes on each side. Remove from skillet; set aside. Repeat with remaining veal, using remaining 3 tablespoons olive oil. Preheat oven to 350° F. Place veal in a shallow 12- x 8- x 2-inch baking pan. Pour tomato sauce over all. Top with mozzarella cheese; sprinkle with remaining 2 tablespoons Parmesan cheese. Bake until hot and bubbly, about 15 minutes. Yield: 4 portions.

Calves Liver Milanese
(Fegato alla Milanese)

Even liver-haters will appreciate this.

1½ pounds calves liver, ¼ inch thick
½ cup flour
2 eggs, lightly beaten
1 cup Progresso Italian-style Bread Crumbs
6 tablespoons Progresso Olive Oil
Lemon wedges

Dredge liver on both sides with flour, then dip in eggs, then in bread crumbs. In a large skillet heat 2 tablespoons of the olive oil until hot. Sauté liver a few pieces at a time, 2 to 3 minutes on each side, adding more olive oil as needed. Do not overcook. Remove liver and keep warm. Repeat with remaining liver. Serve with lemon wedges. Garnish with parsley sprigs, if desired. Yield: 6 portions.

Pork Chops with Peppers
(Costolette di Maiale con Peperoni)

The sweet fried peppers make all the difference here.

2 tablespoons Progresso Olive Oil
6 loin pork chops, about ¾ inch thick
¾ teaspoon salt
¼ teaspoon ground black pepper
2 jars (6 ounces each) Progresso Sweet Fried Peppers
½ cup dry vermouth or white wine
1 teaspoon Italian seasoning

Preheat oven to 450° F. Place olive oil in the bottom of a large shallow baking pan. Sprinkle pork chops with salt and black pepper. Arrange in a single layer in prepared pan. Bake, uncovered, for 20 minutes, turning once. Top chops with sweet fried peppers, wine and Italian seasoning. Reduce oven temperature to 325° F. Bake, uncovered, basting occasionally, until chops are cooked through, about 30 minutes. Yield: 6 portions.

Beef Granatine
(Bistecca Tritata Impanata)

1 pound ground beef
1 cup Progresso Italian-style Bread Crumbs, divided
2 tablespoons Progresso Grated Parmesan Cheese
⅛ teaspoon ground nutmeg
¼ cup milk
2 eggs, lightly beaten, divided
¼ cup Progresso Olive Oil

In a large bowl lightly combine beef, ½ cup of the bread crumbs, Parmesan cheese, nutmeg, milk and half of the beaten eggs. Shape into 4 oval patties. Dip into remaining beaten egg and then into the remaining ½ cup bread crumbs. In a large skillet heat olive oil until hot. Add patties. Cook over low to moderate heat until brown and cooked through, about 6 minutes on each side. Yield: 4 portions.

Beef Rolls with Tomato Sauce
(Braciolette di Manzo Ripiene)

Beef steaks filled and rolled into individual packages. Good for Sunday dinner.

2 pounds boneless round steaks, ½ inch thick
1½ cups Progresso Italian-style Bread Crumbs
¼ cup raisins
¼ cup chopped pignoli (pine nuts)
2 tablespoons chopped fresh parsley
1 egg, lightly beaten
4 tablespoons Progresso Olive Oil, divided
1 can (28 ounces) Progresso Crushed Tomatoes
2 tablespoons Progresso Tomato Paste
1 teaspoon oregano leaves, crushed
½ teaspoon salt
⅛ teaspoon ground black pepper

Between 2 sheets of wax paper with a meat mallet or cleaver pound steaks ¼ inch thick. Cut into 6 portions. In a bowl combine bread crumbs, raisins, pignoli, parsley, egg and 1 tablespoon of the olive oil. Spoon equal amounts of the bread crumb mixture into the middle of each steak. Roll steaks and tie with string or heavy cotton thread. In a large skillet heat remaining 3 tablespoons olive oil until hot. Add beef rolls. Brown on all sides. Add tomatoes, tomato paste, oregano, salt and black pepper. Simmer, covered, until meat is tender, about 2 hours. (If sauce becomes very thick during cooking, stir in a small amount of water or red wine.) Remove strings before serving. Serve with freshly cooked spaghetti, if desired. Yield: 6 portions.

Veal Piccata alla Progresso
(Vitello Piccata alla Progresso)

1½ pounds boneless veal leg, ¼ inch thick (scallopine) or chicken breasts, boned, skinned and halved
1 egg, lightly beaten
1¼ cups Progresso Italian-style Bread Crumbs
½ cup Progresso Olive Oil
¾ cup dry vermouth or white wine
1 tablespoon lemon juice
½ teaspoon salt
⅛ teaspoon ground black pepper

Pound veal between 2 pieces of wax paper with a meat mallet or cleaver until ⅛ inch thick. Dip veal in egg, then in bread crumbs, pressing bread crumbs into meat. Place on a platter. Refrigerate for 30 minutes or freeze for 5 minutes. In a large skillet heat olive oil until hot. Add veal a few pieces at a time. Brown about 2 minutes on each side. Remove from skillet; keep warm. Repeat with remaining veal. Into drippings left in skillet stir wine, lemon juice, salt and black pepper. Bring to a boil. Reduce heat and simmer, uncovered, until sauce is reduced to about ⅓ cup, about 5 minutes. Serve about 1 tablespoon sauce over each piece of veal. Garnish with lemon wedges and chopped parsley, if desired. Yield: 6 portions.

Breaded Pork Chops
(Costolette di Maiale Panate)

8 thin pork chops (about 2 pounds)
½ cup Progresso Wine Vinegar
1 egg
1 tablespoon cold water
1 cup Progresso Italian-style Bread Crumbs
⅓ cup Progresso Olive Oil

Arrange pork chops in a shallow pan. Pour wine vinegar over chops. Cover and refrigerate about 2 hours, turning once. Beat egg with cold water. Dip both sides of each chop in egg mixture, then lightly coat with bread crumbs. In a large skillet heat olive oil until hot. Sauté chops, a few at a time, until browned on both sides and cooked through. Do not crowd. Repeat with remaining pork chops, adding more oil if needed. Yield: 4 portions.

Italian Beef Stew
(Manzo Stufato)

Make this a day ahead to develop flavors. It's pretty served with green fettuccine noodles.

3 tablespoons Progresso Olive Oil
3 pounds boneless beef shoulder or chuck, cut in 2-inch cubes
1 cup chopped onion
4 ounces sliced boiled ham, slivered
1 clove garlic, minced
1 can (28 ounces) Progresso Crushed Tomatoes
2 tablespoons Progresso Wine Vinegar
2 teaspoons basil leaves
2 teaspoons salt
¼ teaspoon ground black pepper
1 can (14 ounces) Progresso Artichoke Hearts
1 package (10 ounces) frozen peas, thawed

Preheat oven to 325° F. In a large ovenproof saucepot heat olive oil until hot. Add beef a few pieces at a time. Brown on all sides about 15 minutes. Remove from saucepot; set aside. Repeat with remaining beef. To saucepot add onion, ham and garlic. Sauté over moderate heat for 2 minutes. Add tomatoes, wine vinegar, basil, salt and black pepper; mix well. Return beef to pot. Cover and bake until beef is fork-tender, about 2½ hours. Strain off fat. Drain artichokes. Add artichoke hearts and peas. Cover and bake 15 minutes longer. Serve with freshly cooked fettuccine noodles, if desired. Yield: 8 portions.

Beef Slices alla Pizzaiola
(Fettine alla Pizzaiola)

Pizzaiola means "with tomatoes." The simple sauce is also good with chicken, fish or meatballs.

2½ pounds boneless top round steak, ½ inch thick
2 eggs, lightly beaten
1¼ cups Progresso Italian-style Bread Crumbs
6 tablespoons Progresso Olive Oil, divided
2 cloves garlic, crushed
1 can (28 ounces) Progresso Crushed Tomatoes
1 jar (6 ounces) Progresso Sweet Fried Peppers
1 teaspoon salt
½ teaspoon Italian seasoning
¼ teaspoon ground black pepper

Between 2 pieces of wax paper with a meat mallet or cleaver pound steaks until about ¼ inch thick. Cut each steak into portion-sized pieces. Dip in eggs, then in bread crumbs. In a large skillet heat 2 tablespoons of the olive oil until hot. Add 2 pieces of steak. Brown 2 to 3 minutes on each side. Remove from skillet; set aside. Repeat with remaining steaks, using remaining 4 tablespoons olive oil. To drippings in skillet add garlic. Sauté for 1 minute. Add tomatoes, sweet fried peppers, salt, Italian seasoning and black pepper. Bring to a boil, stirring to loosen particles from bottom of skillet. Reduce heat and simmer, uncovered, for 5 minutes. Spoon sauce over steaks. Serve with freshly cooked pasta, if desired. Yield: 6 portions.

Beef Slices alla Pizzaiola

Braised Veal Shanks
(Osso Buco)

8 pounds meaty veal shanks, cut in 2-inch
  pieces
½ cup flour
½ cup Progresso Olive Oil
1½ cups thinly sliced onions
1½ cups thinly sliced celery
1 cup thinly sliced carrots
¾ cup dry vermouth or white wine
1 can (28 ounces) Progresso Crushed
  Tomatoes
2 bay leaves
1 teaspoon thyme leaves
1 teaspoon basil leaves
½ teaspoon oregano leaves
1 teaspoon salt
¼ teaspoon ground black pepper
  Gremolata (recipe follows)

Coat veal on all sides with flour. In a large saucepot heat about ¼ cup of the olive oil until hot. Add veal, a few pieces at a time. Sauté until lightly browned on all sides. Remove from saucepot; set aside. Repeat with remaining veal adding more olive oil if needed. Add onions, celery and carrots to saucepot. Sauté until onions are tender, about 5 minutes. With a slotted spoon remove vegetables; set aside. Add wine to saucepot. Cook over moderate heat, stirring to loosen brown particles on bottom. Return veal and juices to pot. Cover with vegetables. Add crushed tomatoes, bay leaves, thyme, basil, oregano, salt and black pepper. Simmer, covered, until veal is tender, about 1¼ hours, basting occasionally. If necessary, uncover during last 15 minutes of cooking to thicken sauce. Remove bay leaves. Sprinkle with Gremolata. Serve with steamed rice or risotto, if desired. Yield: 6 portions.

Gremolata

¼ cup chopped fresh parsley
1 large clove garlic, finely chopped
2 teaspoons grated lemon peel

In a small bowl combine all ingredients. Yield: about 5 tablespoons.

Cold Sliced Veal with Tuna Sauce
(Vitello Tonnato)

This is an unusual and satisfying cold summer dish. Be sure not to add salt to the water when you cook the veal; the anchovies and capers in the sauce furnish the saltiness.

3 pounds boneless veal roast, tied
4 cups water
1 carrot
1 onion, sliced
4 sprigs parsley
1 can (6½ ounces) Progresso Light Tuna
  (Tonno)
1 cup Progresso Olive Oil
¼ cup lemon juice
6 anchovy fillets
3 tablespoons capers
1 cup mayonnaise

In a large saucepot place veal, water, carrot, onion and parsley. Bring to a boil. Reduce heat and simmer, covered, until veal is fork-tender, about 2 hours. Cool meat in broth. Refrigerate until chilled. Remove veal from broth. Remove string; cut veal into thin slices. Arrange slices on a platter. Cover and refrigerate. In the container of an electric blender place tuna, olive oil, lemon juice, anchovies and capers. Cover and blend until smooth. Blend in mayonnaise. Spread about one-third of the sauce in a 12- x 10- x 2-inch casserole or serving dish. Top with half of the veal slices. Repeat layering once more, ending with the sauce. Refrigerate, covered, at least 2 hours before serving. Garnish with olives, lemon slices and parsley sprigs, if desired. Keeps well for several days when well-covered in the refrigerator. Yield: 8 to 10 portions.

Italian Meatloaf
(Polpettone)

1 pound ground beef
¾ cup Progresso Italian-style Bread Crumbs, divided
1 can (8 ounces) Progresso Tomato Sauce
1 egg, lightly beaten
½ teaspoon salt
⅛ teaspoon ground black pepper
3 hard-cooked eggs
2 tablespoons Progresso Olive Oil

Preheat oven to 325° F. In a large bowl combine beef, ½ cup of the bread crumbs, tomato sauce, egg, salt and black pepper. Mix gently but thoroughly. Place about one-half of the meat mixture in the bottom of a 12- x 8- x 2-inch baking pan. Pat into a rectangle approximately 4 inches wide. Place eggs lengthwise down center of meat. Pat remaining meat over eggs to form a rounded loaf. Combine remaining ¼ cup bread crumbs with olive oil. Press evenly over loaf. Bake until cooked through, about 1 hour. Let stand for 5 minutes before slicing. Serve with freshly cooked spaghetti, if desired. Yield: 4 portions.

Piquant Pork Chops
(Costolette di Maiale Piccante)

3 tablespoons flour
¼ teaspoon ground black pepper
6 center-cut pork chops, about 1 inch thick
3 tablespoons Progresso Olive Oil
1 clove garlic, crushed
2 teaspoons mashed anchovies
1½ cups chicken broth
⅓ cup Progresso Wine Vinegar
½ cup drained Progresso Olive Salad (Olive Condite)

Mix flour and black pepper. Coat chops on both sides with flour mixture; set aside. In a large skillet heat olive oil until hot. Add chops, 3 at a time. Brown well on both sides. Remove from skillet; set aside. Discard all but 1 tablespoon of the drippings from the skillet. Add garlic and anchovies; cook and stir for 1 minute. Add chicken broth, wine vinegar and olive salad. Cook over moderate heat, stirring to loosen particles from bottom of skillet. Bring to a boil. Return chops to skillet. Simmer, covered, until chops are tender, about 45 minutes. Or place chops in a 13- x 9-inch shallow baking pan. Pour vinegar mixture over chops. Cover and bake in a preheated 350° F oven until chops are fork-tender, about 45 minutes. Yield: 6 portions.

Pork and Lentil Stew
(Spezzatino di Maiale con Lenticchie)

This hearty winter dish tastes even better the second day.

3 pounds boneless pork shoulder, cut in 1-inch cubes
¼ cup flour
2 teaspoons salt
¼ teaspoon ground black pepper
3 tablespoons Progresso Olive Oil
1 cup chopped onion
1 can (29 ounces) Progresso Tomato Puree
½ cup water
2 cans (19 ounces each) Progresso Lentil Soup
3 cups peeled potatoes in 1-inch chunks
3 cups celery in 2-inch chunks

Coat pork cubes with flour mixed with salt and black pepper. In a large saucepot or skillet heat olive oil until hot. Add a few pieces of the pork. Brown on all sides. Remove from saucepot; set aside. Repeat with remaining pork. Add onion to drippings left in saucepot. Sauté until tender, about 5 minutes. Stir in tomato puree and water, stirring to loosen particles from bottom of skillet. Return pork to saucepot. Bring to a boil. Reduce heat and simmer, covered, for 45 minutes, stirring occasionally. Add lentil soup, potatoes and celery. Return to a boil. Reduce heat and simmer, covered, until pork and vegetables are tender, about 30 minutes, stirring occasionally. Yield: 8 to 10 portions.

Chicken Piccante
(Pollo Piccante)

This is a delicious company dish. The ingredients may be doubled or tripled.

3 pounds chicken parts
¼ cup Progresso Italian-style Bread Crumbs
4 tablespoons Progresso Olive Oil, divided
¾ teaspoon rosemary leaves, crushed
½ teaspoon oregano leaves, crushed
¼ teaspoon crushed red pepper flakes
¼ teaspoon salt
1 cup dry vermouth or white wine
3 cups sliced mushrooms
2 cloves garlic, finely minced
1 jar (7 ounces) Progresso Roasted Peppers
2 teaspoons capers
¼ cup chopped fresh parsley

On a firm surface, pound chicken (bones and all) with a mallet or cleaver until they are as flat as possible. Lightly coat chicken with bread crumbs. In a large skillet heat 2 tablespoons of the olive oil until hot. Add chicken, a few pieces at a time, so they are not crowded. Sauté until brown on all sides. As chicken browns, remove pieces to a plate and reserve. Return chicken to skillet skin side up. Sprinkle with rosemary, oregano, red pepper and salt. Pour wine over all. Simmer, covered, until chicken is cooked, about 35 minutes, basting occasionally. About 10 minutes before chicken is done, in a separate large skillet heat remaining 2 tablespoons olive oil until hot. Add mushrooms and garlic. Sauté until light brown. Cut roasted peppers in strips. Add peppers and capers to mushrooms. Heat until hot. To serve, transfer chicken to a serving platter. Spoon pepper mixture and pan juices over all. Garnish with parsley. Yield: 4 to 6 portions.

Chicken Stew with Cannellini
(Spezzatino di Pollo con Cannellini)

2½ pounds chicken parts
2 teaspoons salt, divided
¼ cup Progresso Olive Oil
1 clove garlic, crushed
1 can (16 ounces) Progresso Crushed Tomatoes
⅓ cup Progresso Wine Vinegar
½ teaspoon basil leaves, crushed
1 can (19 ounces) Progresso Cannellini (White Kidney Beans)

Sprinkle chicken with 1 teaspoon of the salt. In a large skillet heat olive oil until hot. Add chicken, a few pieces at a time, so they are not crowded. Sauté until brown on all sides. Remove to a plate and reserve. Drain off all but 1 tablespoon of the oil. Add garlic. Sauté for 1 minute. Stir in tomatoes, wine vinegar, basil and remaining 1 teaspoon salt. Return chicken to skillet, skin side up. Spoon tomato mixture over chicken. Simmer, covered, until chicken is cooked, about 40 minutes. Drain and rinse cannellini. Add to skillet. Simmer until beans are hot, about 5 minutes. Yield: 4 portions.

Chicken Breasts with Marsala and Peas
(Petti di Pollo alla Marsala con Piselli)

2 whole chicken breasts, boned, skinned and halved
3 tablespoons Progresso Italian-style Bread Crumbs
2 tablespoons Progresso Olive Oil
⅔ cup dry Marsala wine
1 package (10 ounces) frozen peas, thawed

Lightly coat chicken with bread crumbs. In a large skillet heat olive oil until hot. Add chicken. Sauté until brown on both sides. Pour Marsala over chicken. Simmer, covered, for 5 minutes. Turn chicken and add peas. Simmer, covered, until peas are hot and chicken is cooked and tender, about 5 minutes. Yield: 4 portions.

Progresso Chicken Fricassee, page 31
Country Chicken, page 31

Chicken with Lentils and Chick Peas
(Pollo con Lenticchie e Ceci)

3 tablespoons Progresso Olive Oil
2½ pounds chicken parts
2 cans (19 ounces each) Progresso Lentil Soup
½ cup dry vermouth or white wine
¼ teaspoon ground black pepper
1 can (19 ounces) Progresso Chick Peas (Ceci)

In a large skillet heat olive oil until hot. Add chicken. Sauté until brown on all sides. Drain off fat. Stir in lentil soup, wine and black pepper. Bring to a boil. Reduce heat and simmer, covered, until chicken is cooked and tender, about 45 minutes, stirring often and adding a small amount of water, if needed. Drain chick peas; stir into skillet. Heat until hot. Serve sprinkled with parsley, if desired. Yield: 4 portions.

Chicken and Sausage Pizzaiola
(Pollo alla Pizzaiola con Salsiccie)

12 ounces sweet Italian sausage links
1 tablespoon Progresso Olive Oil
2 cups sliced onions separated into rings
2 large cloves garlic, finely minced
3 pounds chicken parts
1 can (28 ounces) Progresso Crushed Tomatoes
1 large bay leaf
1½ teaspoons basil leaves
1 teaspoon oregano leaves
½ teaspoon salt
⅛ teaspoon ground black pepper
1 jar (7 ounces) Progresso Roasted Peppers

With fork tines pierce sausages in several places. In a large skillet heat olive oil until hot. Add sausages. Cook over low heat, turning frequently, until brown on all sides. Remove sausages to a paper towel; reserve. Pour off all but about 3 tablespoons fat from skillet. (If necessary, add olive oil to make 3 tablespoons.) Add onions and garlic. Sauté until onions are light brown, stirring to loosen particles from the bottom of the skillet. With a slotted spoon, remove onions. Add chicken to the skillet, a few pieces at a time, until brown on all sides. As chicken browns, remove to a plate and reserve. Return chicken to skillet skin side up. Arrange sausages and onions over and around chicken. Pour tomatoes over all. Add bay leaf, basil, oregano, salt and black pepper. Simmer, covered, until chicken is cooked and tender, 35 to 40 minutes, basting occasionally. Cut roasted peppers in strips; add to skillet. Increase heat and cook, uncovered, until the sauce is slightly reduced. Remove bay leaf and serve in shallow bowls. Yield: 6 to 8 portions.

Chicken Breasts with Lemon and Parsley
(Petti di Pollo al Limone con Prezzemolo)

Quickly made and so good. If you prefer even more tartness, squeeze on lemon juice at the table. But taste the chicken first.

⅓ cup dry vermouth or white wine
⅓ cup lemon juice
2 cloves garlic, finely minced
2 whole chicken breasts, boned, skinned and halved
3 tablespoons Progresso Italian-style Bread Crumbs
2 tablespoons Progresso Olive Oil
¼ cup chopped fresh parsley

In a measuring cup combine wine, lemon juice and garlic. Place each chicken breast between 2 pieces of wax paper. Pound with a mallet or cleaver to about ¼ inch thick. Lightly coat chicken with bread crumbs. In a large skillet heat olive oil until hot. Add chicken. Sauté until brown on both sides, about 5 minutes. Stir wine mixture again and pour over chicken. Simmer, uncovered, until chicken is cooked, about 5 minutes. Sprinkle with parsley. Serve with pan juices. Yield: 4 portions.

Tuscan Chicken Breasts
(Petti di Pollo alla Toscana)

A delectable combination of flavors. Be sure to use fresh parsley for garnish.

2 whole chicken breasts, boned, skinned and halved
2 tablespoons flour
1 egg, lightly beaten
1 tablespoon water
5 tablespoons Progresso Italian-style Bread Crumbs
2 tablespoons Progresso Olive Oil
½ teaspoon rosemary leaves, crushed
⅔ cup dry vermouth or white wine
2 cups sliced fresh mushrooms
¼ cup diced Progresso Tuscan Peppers
½ cup chopped fresh parsley

Lightly coat chicken on both sides with flour. Mix egg with water. Dip chicken in egg mixture and then coat with bread crumbs. Refrigerate, uncovered, about 1 hour. In a large skillet heat olive oil until hot. Add chicken. Sauté until brown on both sides. Add rosemary and wine. Simmer, covered, for 5 minutes. Scatter mushrooms over the chicken. Simmer, covered, until chicken and mushrooms are cooked and tender, about 10 minutes. Add Tuscan peppers. Increase the heat, tip the skillet and baste chicken with pan juices until peppers are hot. If necessary, add a little more wine for basting. Serve garnished with parsley. Yield: 4 portions.

Chicken Livers with Peppers and Artichokes
(Fegatini di Pollo con Peperoni e Carciofi)

The nip of wine vinegar at the end adds just the right touch.

4 tablespoons Progresso Olive Oil, divided
1 cup thinly sliced onion separated into rings
1 pound chicken livers, halved
4 tablespoons Progresso Italian-style Bread Crumbs
1 can (14 ounces) Progresso Artichoke Hearts
1 jar (7 ounces) Progresso Roasted Peppers
2 tablespoons Progresso Wine Vinegar

In a large skillet heat 1 tablespoon of the olive oil until hot. Add onion. Sauté until brown. With a slotted spoon remove to a plate and reserve. Pat livers dry with paper towels. Lightly coat livers with bread crumbs. In the skillet heat remaining 3 tablespoons olive oil until hot. Add livers. Sauté over high heat until brown, about 5 minutes. Do not overcook. Remove to plate. Return onion to skillet. Drain and halve artichoke hearts. Cut roasted peppers in strips. Add artichoke hearts, peppers and wine vinegar to skillet. Cook over high heat until artichokes are hot, mixing gently and loosening any particles in the bottom of the skillet. Spoon over livers. Yield: 4 portions.

Fried Chicken Milanese
(Pollo alla Milanese)

3 pounds chicken parts
1 egg
2 tablespoons water
4 tablespoons flour
½ cup Progresso Italian-style Bread Crumbs
3 tablespoons Progresso Olive Oil
Lemon wedges

On a firm surface pound chicken parts (bones and all) with a mallet or cleaver until they are as flat as possible. Mix egg with water. Lightly coat chicken with flour. Dip chicken in egg and then coat with bread crumbs. Arrange chicken in a single layer on a platter. Refrigerate, uncovered, about 1 hour. In a large skillet heat olive oil until hot. Add chicken. Cook until golden brown on both sides. Reduce heat and fry, uncovered, until chicken is cooked and tender, 35 to 40 minutes, turning occasionally. Serve with lemon wedges. Yield: 4 portions.

Progresso Chicken Fricassee
(Pollo alla Fricassea)

Particularly good for company, this can be prepared ahead and reheated.

3 tablespoons Progresso Olive Oil, divided
2 cups coarsely chopped onions
2 cups thinly sliced carrots
2 cups sliced mushrooms
3 pounds chicken parts
1½ teaspoons basil leaves, crushed
1 teaspoon thyme leaves, crushed
½ teaspoon salt
⅛ teaspoon ground black pepper
1 can (28 ounces) Progresso Crushed Tomatoes
1 jar (6 ounces) Progresso Sweet Fried Peppers, undrained

In a large saucepot heat 2 tablespoons of the olive oil until hot. Add onions, carrots and mushrooms. Sauté until vegetables are barely tender. With a slotted spoon remove vegetables to a plate and reserve. Heat remaining 1 tablespoon oil in saucepot. Add chicken, a few pieces at a time, so they are not crowded. Sauté until brown on all sides. As chicken browns, remove to a plate and reserve. Return chicken, skin side up, to saucepot. Cover with vegetables. Sprinkle with basil, thyme, salt and black pepper. Add tomatoes and sweet fried peppers. Simmer, covered, until chicken is cooked and tender, about 40 minutes, basting occasionally with sauce. Garnish with parsley, if desired. Yield: 4 portions.

Italian Roast Stuffed Chicken
(Pollo Arrosto Ripieno)

3 tablespoons butter
1½ cups chopped onions
1½ cups chopped celery
1½ cups chopped mushrooms
¾ cup Progresso Italian-style Bread Crumbs
¼ cup chopped fresh parsley
½ teaspoon rosemary leaves, crushed
⅓ cup dry vermouth or white wine
5 pound roasting chicken

Preheat oven to 350° F. In a large skillet melt butter. Add onions, celery and mushrooms. Sauté until onions are tender and liquid from mushrooms evaporates, about 5 minutes. Remove from heat. Add bread crumbs, parsley, rosemary and wine. Mix gently until blended. Stuff body cavity of chicken with crumb-vegetable mixture; close with skewers. Place chicken in a roasting pan. Roast, uncovered, until cooked and tender, about 2½ hours, or when a meat thermometer inserted in the thigh reaches 185° F. Remove chicken from oven and let rest 10 to 15 minutes before carving. Yield: 6 portions (about ½ cup stuffing per portion).

Country Chicken
(Pollo alla Contadina)

In Italy they make this dish with veal; we've substituted less expensive chicken breasts.

2 whole chicken breasts, boned, skinned and halved
3 tablespoons Progresso Italian-style Bread Crumbs
2 tablespoons Progresso Olive Oil
1 can (19 ounces) Progresso Minestrone Soup
2 tablespoons Progresso Wine Vinegar
⅛ teaspoon sugar
1 can (14 ounces) Progresso Artichoke Hearts
½ cup chopped fresh parsley

Lightly coat chicken on both sides with bread crumbs. In a large skillet heat olive oil until hot. Add chicken. Sauté until brown on both sides. Combine minestrone soup, wine vinegar and sugar. Pour over chicken. Simmer, covered, until chicken is cooked and tender, about 10 minutes. Drain artichokes; cut in halves. Add to skillet. Increase the heat and baste artichokes with pan juices until artichokes are hot. Serve over freshly cooked spaghetti, if desired. Yield: 4 portions.

Pork and Lentil Stew, page 25

Tuscan Seafood Stew
(Cacciucco alla Livornese)

2 live lobsters (about 1¼ pounds each)
¼ cup Progresso Olive Oil
¾ cup chopped onion
2 cloves garlic, minced
1 can (10½ ounces) Progresso Red Clam
   Sauce
½ cup dry vermouth or white wine
1 teaspoon grated lemon peel
¾ teaspoon salt
8 ounces halibut steak, cut in chunks
8 ounces flounder fillets, cut in chunks
8 ounces scallops
¼ cup chopped fresh parsley

Cut tails from each lobster; cut in halves lengthwise. Cut large claws from body. Remove and discard antennae and split body sections lengthwise, removing and discarding stomachs and intestines. Reserve lobster. In a large saucepot heat olive oil until hot. Add onion and garlic. Sauté for 3 minutes. Add red clam sauce, wine, lemon peel and salt. Bring to a boil. Reduce heat and simmer, uncovered, for 5 minutes. Add halibut and reserved lobster. Simmer, covered, for 5 minutes. Add flounder and scallops. Simmer, covered, 5 minutes longer. With a slotted spoon place seafood in large tureen. Stir parsley into sauce. Pour over fish. Yield: 6 portions.

Fish Rolls with Vegetables and Clam Sauce
(Involtini di Pesce al Vongole)

Water
1½ pounds fish fillets
½ cup thinly sliced zucchini
½ cup thinly sliced carrot
½ cup onion rings
1 can (10½ ounces) Progresso White Clam
   Sauce
½ cup diced tomato

In a large skillet bring ½-inch water to a boil. Roll each fish fillet from the narrow end; secure with a toothpick. Place in a skillet along with zucchini, carrot and onion. Simmer, covered, until fish flakes easily with a fork and vegetables are tender, about 3 minutes. With a slotted spoon remove fish and vegetables to a serving platter containing a bed of freshly cooked pasta or rice, if desired; cover to keep warm. Discard liquid in skillet. Add clam sauce and tomato to skillet. Simmer, uncovered, until tomato is softened, about 1 minute. Spoon sauce over fish. Yield: 4 to 6 portions.

Baked Lobster with Clam Stuffing
(Aragosta Ripiene al Forno)

2 live lobsters, 2 pounds each
1 cup Progresso Italian-style Bread Crumbs
1 can (10½ ounces) Progresso White Clam
   Sauce
2 tablespoons dry vermouth or white wine
2 tablespoons Progresso Olive Oil
   Melted butter

Preheat oven to 425° F. Split each lobster from head to end of tail. Remove and discard stomach and intestinal vein. Remove and reserve tomalley, if desired. In a medium bowl combine bread crumbs, clam sauce, wine and tomalley. Place lobsters in a large, shallow baking pan, spreading open as far as possible. Fill lobster cavities with clam stuffing, mounding slightly. Drizzle olive oil over stuffing. Place a stone or potato on the end of each tail to weight it down. Add enough water to cover the bottom of the pan. Bake, uncovered, until lobsters are bright red and the top of the stuffing is lightly browned, 20 to 25 minutes. Serve with melted butter. Yield: 2 portions.

Shrimp in Clam Sauce
(Scampi con Vongole)

2 tablespoons Progresso Olive Oil
1 pound large, peeled and deveined shrimp
1 can (10½ ounces) Progresso White Clam Sauce
¼ teaspoon oregano leaves, crushed
1 tablespoon lemon juice
3 tablespoons Progresso Italian-style Bread Crumbs

In a large skillet heat olive oil until hot. Add shrimp. Sauté just until shrimp turn opaque. Do not overcook. Add white clam sauce, oregano and lemon juice. Sprinkle bread crumbs evenly over shrimp. Cook over high heat, basting shrimp with sauce, until sauce is slightly thickened, about 1 minute. Serve over steamed rice, if desired. Yield: 3 to 4 portions.

Broiled Shellfish Venetian Style
(Frutta di Mare alla Veneziana)

Serve with plenty of lemon wedges at your next company dinner.

1 pound peeled and deveined shrimp
1 pound sea scallops
⅔ cup Progresso Italian-style Bread Crumbs
¼ cup Progresso Olive Oil
Lemon wedges

Place shrimp and scallops in a large bowl. In a small bowl combine bread crumbs and olive oil. Spoon over fish. Mix gently to coat fish with crumb mixture. Cover and refrigerate about 1 hour. Place broiler rack 3 inches from heat source. Preheat broiler to hot. Line broiler pan with aluminum foil. Thread fish on skewers. Place fish on a rack in the broiler pan. Broil, turning twice, until crisp and golden on all sides, about 5 minutes. Do not overcook. Serve with lemon wedges. Yield: 6 to 8 portions.

Fillet of Sole Milanese
(Sogliola alla Milanese)

1 pound sole fillets (or other fish fillets)
¼ cup flour
1 egg
2 tablespoons water
⅔ cup Progresso Italian-style Bread Crumbs
4 tablespoons butter, divided
4 lemon wedges

Lightly coat fish with flour. Mix egg with water. Dip fish in egg mixture and coat with bread crumbs. In a large skillet melt 3 tablespoons of the butter. Add as many of the fillets as will fit comfortably in a single layer. Sauté over moderate heat until golden on both sides, about 3 minutes, turning once. Remove to a platter. Cover to keep warm. Repeat with remaining fish and butter. Serve with lemon wedges. Yield: 3 to 4 portions.

Swordfish Sicilian Style
(Pesce Spada alla Siracusa)

1½ pounds swordfish steaks, 1 inch thick
¼ cup Progresso Italian-style Bread Crumbs
3 tablespoons Progresso Olive Oil
½ cup drained Progresso Pepper Salad
⅓ cup dry vermouth or white wine
½ cup chopped fresh parsley

Coat swordfish on both sides with bread crumbs. In a large skillet heat olive oil until hot. Add fish. Sauté until lightly browned on both sides. Turn heat to low. Spoon pepper salad over fish; pour wine over all. Simmer, covered, until fish flakes easily with a fork, about 5 minutes. Transfer fish to serving plates. Cover to keep warm. Bring pan juices to a boil; boil 1 to 2 minutes, stirring to loosen browned particles on bottom. Spoon over fish. Sprinkle with parsley. Yield: 6 portions.

Fish with Clams and Peppers
(Pesce con Vongole e Peperoni)

The clam sauce adds an extra taste of the sea to this simple fish dish.

1 pound fish steaks, ½ inch thick
1 can (10½ ounces) Progresso White Clam Sauce
½ cup dry vermouth or white wine
½ teaspoon basil leaves, crushed
½ teaspoon salt
½ cup green pepper in matchstick-sized pieces
½ cup diced Progresso Roasted Peppers

In a large skillet bring 1 inch water to a boil. Add fish. Reduce heat and simmer, covered, until fish flakes easily with a fork, 4 to 5 minutes. Remove fish; set aside and keep warm. To same skillet add clam sauce, wine, basil, salt and green pepper. Bring to a boil. Reduce heat and simmer, covered, until green pepper is tender, 4 to 5 minutes. Stir in roasted peppers. Heat until hot. Spoon sauce over fish. Serve with steamed rice, spooning remaining sauce over rice, if desired. Yield: 4 portions.

Halibut with Saffron Crumb Topping
(Pesce da Taglio Briciolata al Forno)

2 pounds halibut or swordfish steaks
3 tablespoons Progresso Olive Oil
2 cloves garlic, minced
½ cup Progresso Italian-style Bread Crumbs
¼ cup chopped fresh parsley
½ teaspoon saffron, crushed

Preheat oven to 375° F. Place fish in an oiled 12- x 8- x 2-inch baking pan. In a small saucepan heat olive oil until hot. Add garlic. Sauté for 1 minute. Remove from heat. Stir in bread crumbs, parsley and saffron. Sprinkle over halibut. Bake until fish flakes easily with a fork and crumb topping is golden, about 20 minutes. Yield: 6 portions.

Baked Fish Sicilian Style
(Pesce al Forno alla Siciliana)

2 pounds swordfish or halibut steaks
2 tablespoons Progresso Olive Oil
1 cup chopped onion
1 can (28 ounces) Progresso Crushed Tomatoes
½ cup Progresso Olive Salad (Olive Condite), undrained
½ cup chopped fresh parsley

Preheat oven to 375° F. Place fish in an oiled 12- x 8- x 2-inch baking pan. In a large skillet heat olive oil until hot. Add onion. Sauté for 2 minutes. Stir in tomatoes and olive salad. Bring to a boil. Reduce heat and simmer, uncovered, until sauce is slightly thickened, about 10 minutes. Pour sauce over fish. Bake, uncovered, until fish flakes easily with a fork, about 20 minutes. Sprinkle with parsley. Serve with steamed rice, if desired. Yield: 6 portions.

Tuna Croquettes
(Crochette di Tonno)

2 cans (6½ ounces each) Progresso Light Tuna (Tonno)
2 eggs, lightly beaten
½ cup Progresso Italian-style Bread Crumbs
¼ cup chopped fresh parsley
About 1 cup Progresso Olive Oil

Drain and flake tuna. Combine tuna, eggs, bread crumbs and parsley. Shape into 1½-inch balls. In a large skillet heat olive oil until hot. Add tuna balls a few at a time. Brown on all sides, about 5 minutes. Drain on paper towels. Serve hot. Yield: about 2 dozen.

Scallops and Red Peppers
(Canestrelli e Peperoni Briciolati)

If you use the larger sea scallops for this, cut them in halves or quarters.

4 tablespoons Progresso Olive Oil
1 pound bay scallops
1 large clove garlic, finely minced
½ teaspoon oregano leaves, crushed
¼ teaspoon salt
⅛ teaspoon ground black pepper
⅓ cup chopped Progresso Roasted Peppers
3 tablespoons chopped fresh parsley
4 tablespoons Progresso Italian-style Bread Crumbs, divided
1 tablespoon lemon juice

Preheat broiler to hot. Butter individual casseroles or one 9-inch pie pan. In a large skillet heat olive oil until hot. Add scallops, garlic, oregano, salt and black pepper. Sauté over high heat for 3 minutes. Remove from heat. Add roasted peppers, parsley, 2 tablespoons of the bread crumbs and lemon juice; mix gently. Place in prepared casseroles or pie pan. Sprinkle with remaining 2 tablespoons bread crumbs. Place under broiler until lightly browned. Yield: 3 to 4 portions.

Shrimp and Clams Peasant Style
(Gamberi e Vongole alla Contadina)

¼ cup Progresso Olive Oil
4 cloves garlic, minced
2 pounds peeled and deveined shrimp
1 jar (7 ounces) Progresso Roasted Peppers, chopped
⅓ cup Progresso Italian-style Bread Crumbs
½ teaspoon salt
¼ teaspoon ground black pepper
1 can (10½ ounces) Progresso Red Clam Sauce
½ cup dry vermouth or white wine
⅓ cup chopped fresh parsley

In a large skillet heat olive oil until hot. Add garlic. Sauté for 1 minute. Stir in shrimp, roasted peppers, bread crumbs, salt, black pepper, clam sauce and wine. Bring to a boil. Reduce heat and simmer, covered, until shrimp turn opaque, about 4 minutes. Stir in parsley. Serve over steamed rice, if desired. Yield: 6 portions.

Cold Pepper Stuffed Fillet of Sole
(Involtini di Sogliola)

½ cup finely chopped Progresso Roasted Peppers
1½ pounds sole or other fish fillets
¼ cup dry vermouth or white wine
2 tablespoons Progresso Olive Oil
1½ teaspoons salt, divided
⅛ teaspoon ground black pepper
2 medium cucumbers, peeled and thinly sliced
¼ cup chopped fresh parsley

Place about 1 tablespoon of the roasted peppers along the short edge of each fillet. Roll up; set aside. In a medium skillet bring wine, olive oil, ½ teaspoon of the salt and black pepper to a boil. Add fish rolls. Reduce heat and simmer, covered, until fish flakes easily with a fork, about 5 minutes. Cover and refrigerate until chilled. Meanwhile, place cucumbers in a small bowl. Sprinkle with remaining 1 teaspoon salt. Let stand for 1 hour. Rinse and drain well. Stir in parsley. Arrange cucumbers on a serving platter. Cut each fish roll crosswise into 4 slices. Arrange around cucumbers. Serve cold. Yield: 6 portions.

Beans Florentine Style, page 39
Stuffed Zucchini, page 39

VEGETABLES, BEANS & RICE

Baked Chick Peas with Sausage
(Ceci e Salsiccie al Forno)

1 pound sweet Italian sausage links
¾ cup thinly sliced green pepper strips
½ cup chopped onion
1 large clove garlic, minced
2 cans (19 ounces each) Progresso Chick
 Peas (Ceci)
1 can (15 ounces) Progresso Tomato Sauce
2 tablespoons chopped fresh parsley
1¼ teaspoons salt
⅛ teaspoon ground black pepper

Preheat oven to 325° F. Cut sausage into ½-inch-thick slices. In a large skillet cook sausage until brown on all sides, about 5 minutes, stirring frequently. Add green pepper, onion and garlic. Cook and stir until tender, about 5 minutes. Stir in chick peas, tomato sauce, parsley, salt and black pepper. Bring to a boil. Turn into a 2-quart casserole. Cover and bake for 30 minutes. Yield: 6 portions.

Quick Eggplant Stuffed Zucchini
(Zucchini Ripieni di Melanzana)

2 medium zucchini (about 1 pound)
 Water
 Salt
1 can (7½ ounces) Progresso Eggplant
 Appetizer (Caponata)
⅓ cup Progresso Italian-style Bread Crumbs
½ cup Progresso Grated Parmesan Cheese

Preheat oven to 350° F. In a large covered skillet cook zucchini in 1-inch boiling water until barely tender, about 5 minutes. Remove zucchini from water; cool slightly. Cut in halves lengthwise. Carefully scoop out centers leaving ¼-inch-thick shells. Lightly sprinkle shells with salt; set aside. Chop pulp. In a small bowl combine pulp with eggplant appetizer and bread crumbs. Spoon into zucchini shells. Sprinkle 2 tablespoons Parmesan cheese over each. Place in a greased shallow baking pan. Bake, uncovered, until shells are tender, about 25 minutes. Yield: 4 portions.

Peppers Roman Style
(Peperoni alla Romana)

Good with an omelet or frittata.

1 tablespoon Progresso Olive Oil
1 large clove garlic, minced
2 jars (6 ounces each) Progresso Sweet Fried
 Peppers
2 cups peeled and coarsely chopped fresh
 tomatoes
1 teaspoon basil leaves, crushed
⅛ teaspoon ground black pepper
¼ cup chopped fresh parsley

In a small skillet heat olive oil until hot. Add garlic. Sauté for 1 minute. Stir in sweet fried peppers, tomatoes, basil and black pepper. Cook and stir over moderate heat until tomatoes are softened, about 5 minutes. Stir in parsley. Yield: 4 portions.

Potatoes Palermo
(Patate alla Palermo)

3 medium potatoes, peeled and thinly sliced (6 cups)
¼ cup chopped green pepper
¼ cup chopped onion
¼ teaspoon salt
1 can (10½ ounces) Progresso White Clam Sauce

Preheat oven to 350° F. Place potatoes in a 1½-quart baking pan. Sprinkle with green pepper, onion and salt. Pour white clam sauce over all. Cover and bake until potatoes are tender, about 45 minutes. Sprinkle with chopped parsley, if desired. Yield: 4 portions.

Beans Florentine Style
(Fagioli alla Fiorentina)

This may be served as a vegetarian main dish, or along with Pork Chops with Peppers.

1 can (15 ounces) Progresso Tomato Sauce
1 tablespoon Progresso Olive Oil
¾ teaspoon sage leaves, crushed
½ teaspoon salt
⅛ teaspoon ground black pepper
1 large clove garlic, crushed
1 can (19 ounces) Progresso Cannellini (White Kidney Beans)
1 can (19 ounces) Progresso Chick Peas (Ceci)
2 tablespoons Progresso Grated Parmesan Cheese

In a medium saucepan combine tomato sauce, olive oil, sage, salt, black pepper and garlic. Bring to a boil. Reduce heat and simmer, covered, for 5 minutes. Drain cannellini and chick peas. Add to saucepan. Simmer, covered, until beans are hot, about 5 minutes. Serve sprinkled with Parmesan cheese. Yield: 6 to 8 portions.

Stuffed Zucchini
(Zucchini Ripieni di Manzo)

The stuffed zucchini can be prepared ahead and refrigerated, covered, until baking time.

4 medium zucchini (about 2 pounds)
1 pound ground beef
½ cup Progresso Italian-style Bread Crumbs
⅓ cup Progresso Grated Parmesan Cheese
1 teaspoon oregano leaves, crushed
½ teaspoon salt
⅛ teaspoon ground black pepper
1 jar (32 ounces) Progresso Marinara Spaghetti Sauce, divided
1 egg, lightly beaten
⅓ cup shredded mozzarella cheese

Preheat oven to 375° F. Trim ends of zucchini. Cut in halves lengthwise. Carefully scoop out centers leaving ¼-inch-thick shells. Chop pulp (makes about 1 cup); set aside. Heat a large skillet until hot. Add beef. Cook and stir until brown. Pour off fat. Stir in reserved zucchini pulp, bread crumbs, Parmesan cheese, oregano, salt, black pepper, ½ cup of the marinara sauce and egg; mix well. Place zucchini shells in a shallow baking pan. Spoon meat mixture into shells. Pour remaining marinara sauce over and around zucchini. Cover and bake until zucchini shells are tender, 30 to 35 minutes. Sprinkle with mozzarella cheese. Bake, uncovered, until cheese melts, about 5 minutes. Yield: 4 portions.

Eggplant Parmesan
(Melanzana alla Parmigiana)

1 large eggplant (about 1½ pounds)
2 eggs, lightly beaten
1 cup Progresso Italian-style Bread Crumbs
9 tablespoons Progresso Olive Oil, divided
1 large clove garlic, minced
1 can (28 ounces) Progresso Crushed
  Tomatoes
2 teaspoons oregano leaves, crushed
½ cup Progresso Grated Parmesan Cheese,
  divided
8 ounces mozzarella cheese, sliced or
  shredded

Preheat oven to 350° F. Remove stem end of eggplant. Cut unpeeled eggplant into ½-inch-thick slices. Dip in eggs and then in bread crumbs. In a large skillet heat 2 tablespoons of the olive oil until hot. Add eggplant, a few pieces at a time. Sauté until brown, about 2 minutes on each side. Add more olive oil as needed. Remove all eggplant from skillet. In the same skillet heat 1 tablespoon of the olive oil until hot. Add garlic. Sauté for 1 minute. Add crushed tomatoes and oregano. Bring to a boil. Spoon about 1 cup of the tomatoes into a 13- x 9- x 2-inch casserole. Cover with half of the eggplant. Sprinkle with ¼ cup of the Parmesan cheese. Top with about 1 cup of the tomatoes, remaining eggplant, then remaining tomatoes. Cover with mozzarella cheese and sprinkle with remaining ¼ cup Parmesan cheese. Bake, uncovered, until bubbly and golden, about 25 minutes.

Stuffed Tomatoes
(Pomodori Ripieni)

Pile the stuffing high; it won't overflow.

6 large ripe tomatoes
1 package (10 ounces) frozen chopped
  spinach, thawed
3 tablespoons Progresso Olive Oil
¾ cup finely chopped onion
½ cup Progresso Italian-style Bread Crumbs
½ teaspoon salt
⅛ teaspoon ground black pepper
2 tablespoons Progresso Grated Parmesan
  Cheese

Preheat oven to 375° F. Cut a ½-inch slice from the top of each tomato. Carefully scoop out pulp. Chop pulp and set aside. Place tomato shells upside down to drain. Squeeze out as much liquid from spinach as possible; set aside. In a skillet heat olive oil until hot. Add onion. Sauté for 2 minutes. Stir in bread crumbs, salt, black pepper, reserved chopped tomato and spinach. Cook and stir until hot. Spoon into tomato shells, piling high. Sprinkle each stuffed tomato with 1 teaspoon Parmesan cheese. Place in an oiled 10- x 6- x 2-inch baking pan. Bake, uncovered, until tomatoes are soft, about 30 minutes. Yield: 6 portions.

Beans and Bacon in Red Wine
(Fagioli al Vino Rosso)

8 ounces sliced bacon, diced
½ cup chopped onion
2 cans (19 ounces each) Progresso Red
  Kidney Beans or Cannellini (White
  Kidney Beans)
½ cup dry red wine
⅛ teaspoon ground black pepper
¼ cup chopped fresh parsley

In large skillet cook and stir bacon until crisp. Pour off all but about 1 tablespoon of the drippings. Add onion to bacon in skillet. Cook and stir until onion is transparent, about 2 minutes. Drain kidney beans. Stir kidney beans, wine and black pepper into skillet. Bring to a boil. Reduce heat and simmer, uncovered, for 5 minutes. Stir in parsley. Yield: 4 portions.

Rice Balls and Mozzarella
(Crochette di Riso)

2 cups cold cooked rice
½ cup Progresso Grated Parmesan Cheese
¼ cup finely chopped Progresso Roasted
   Peppers
1 egg, lightly beaten
½ teaspoon salt
¼ teaspoon ground black pepper
2 ounces mozzarella cheese
½ cup Progresso Italian-style Bread Crumbs
   Progresso Olive Oil for deep frying

In a medium bowl combine rice, Parmesan cheese, roasted peppers, egg, salt and black pepper. Shape into 2- to 3-inch balls. Cut mozzarella cheese into ½-inch cubes. Make a hole in the middle of each ball and fill with a cheese cube. Re-shape rice mixture to close hole. Roll in bread crumbs. Heat olive oil to 365° F.* Fry rice balls in oil until golden on all sides, about 5 minutes. Remove with a slotted spoon. Drain on paper towels. Serve hot. Yield: 4 portions (8 balls).
*To test for temperature, drop a 1-inch bread cube into hot oil. It will brown in 1 minute if the temperature is about 365° F.

Broccoli with Olive Oil and Lemon
(Broccoli al Olio e Limone)

A refreshing first course, vegetable or salad. Serve chilled or at room temperature.

1 bunch broccoli (1¼ pounds)
   Boiling water
⅓ cup Progresso Olive Oil
3 tablespoons lemon juice
¾ teaspoon salt
1/16 teaspoon ground black pepper

Trim broccoli, cutting away and discarding tough portion of stems. Cut broccoli lengthwise into 1-inch-wide strips. Cook broccoli in a medium-sized covered saucepan in ½-inch boiling water until stem portion is just crisp-tender, 5 to 7 minutes. Drain. Place broccoli in a serving bowl. In a measuring cup combine olive oil, lemon juice, salt and black pepper. Pour over broccoli, turning to coat completely. Cover and refrigerate 2 to 4 hours, spooning olive oil mixture over broccoli occasionally. Yield: 4 to 6 portions.

Artichoke Flan
(Pasticcio di Carciofi)

2 frozen 9-inch pie shells
8 ounces sliced bacon, diced
¾ cup chopped onion
6 eggs
1 cup heavy cream
½ cup milk
1 cup Progresso Grated Parmesan Cheese
1 teaspoon basil leaves, crushed
½ teaspoon salt
¼ teaspoon ground black pepper
1 can (14 ounces) Progresso Artichoke
   Hearts

Preheat oven to 425° F. Prick bottom and sides of pie shells. Bake for 8 minutes. Remove from oven; cool. Reduce oven temperature to 350° F. In a large skillet cook and stir bacon until crisp. Pour off all but 2 tablespoons of the drippings. Add onion. Sauté for 2 minutes. In a medium bowl combine eggs, cream, milk, Parmesan cheese, basil, salt and black pepper. Drain artichoke hearts; cut in halves. Place in reserved pie shells. Sprinkle with onion and bacon. Pour egg mixture over all. Bake until a knife inserted in the center comes out clean, about 35 minutes. Yield: 12 portions.

EGGS & CHEESE

Clam Frittata
(Frittata al Vongole)

1 can (10½ ounces) Progresso White Clam
    Sauce
6 eggs, lightly beaten
¼ cup chopped fresh parsley
⅛ teaspoon ground black pepper
2 tablespoons Progresso Olive Oil

Drain white clam sauce, reserving ⅓ cup of the liquid (use remaining liquid in soup or sauce). In a medium bowl beat eggs, parsley, black pepper, reserved clams and clam liquid until blended. In a medium skillet heat olive oil until hot. Add egg mixture. Cook over low heat until edge is set. With a spatula gently lift edge and tip skillet to allow uncooked egg to flow to the bottom. Cook until golden, about 4 minutes. Turn out onto a plate. Return to skillet top side down. Cook until bottom is golden, about 2 minutes. Cut into wedges. Yield: 4 portions.

Zucchini Frittata
(Frittata con Ricotta e Zucchini)

Ricotta cheese gives this frittata extra protein.

6 eggs, lightly beaten
1 cup ricotta cheese
½ cup Progresso Grated Parmesan Cheese
½ teaspoon salt, divided
⅛ teaspoon ground black pepper
5 tablespoons Progresso Olive Oil
4 cups thinly sliced zucchini
½ cup thinly sliced onion

In a medium bowl beat eggs, ricotta cheese, Parmesan cheese, ¼ teaspoon of the salt and black pepper until blended; set aside. In a medium skillet heat olive oil until hot. Add zucchini, onion and remaining ¼ teaspoon salt. Sauté until zucchini is softened, about 5 minutes. Add egg mixture. Cook over medium heat until bottom is lightly browned, about 6 minutes. Loosen edges with a spatula. Turn out onto a plate. Return to skillet top side down. Cook until bottom is golden, about 2 minutes. To serve, cut into wedges. Yield: 4 portions.

Country Style Omelet
(Frittata Rustica)

4 tablespoons Progresso Olive Oil
½ cup diced zucchini
⅓ cup coarsely chopped celery
6 eggs, lightly beaten
⅓ cup Progresso Grated Parmesan Cheese
⅓ cup chopped Progresso Roasted Peppers
1 teaspoon basil leaves, crushed
¼ teaspoon salt
⅛ teaspoon ground white pepper

In a large skillet heat olive oil until hot. Add zucchini and celery. Sauté for 3 minutes. In a medium bowl beat eggs, Parmesan cheese, roasted peppers, basil, salt and white pepper until blended. Pour over vegetables. Cook over low heat until edge is set. With a spatula gently lift edge and tip skillet to allow uncooked egg to flow to the bottom. Cook until bottom is golden, about 4 minutes. Loosen edges with a spatula. Turn out onto a plate. Return to skillet, top side down. Cook until bottom is golden, about 4 minutes. To serve, cut into wedges. Yield: 4 portions.

Vegetable Frittata
(Frittata di Legumi)

1 jar (3¾ ounces) **Progresso Marinated Mushrooms**
1 cup **thawed frozen asparagus cuts and tips**
7 **eggs, lightly beaten**
¼ cup **Progresso Italian-style Bread Crumbs**
2 tablespoons **water**
¼ teaspoon **salt**
⅛ teaspoon **ground black pepper**
2 tablespoons **Progresso Olive Oil**
1 tablespoon **butter**

Preheat broiler to hot. Drain mushrooms (use marinating liquid in a salad dressing or other recipe). Pat asparagus dry with paper towels. In a large bowl beat eggs, bread crumbs, water, salt and black pepper until blended. In a medium skillet with an ovenproof handle heat olive oil and butter until hot. Pour egg mixture into skillet. Place asparagus and mushrooms over all. Cover with a tight-fitting lid. Cook frittata over medium-low heat until the bottom is golden and top is almost set, about 10 minutes. Place skillet under broiler until top is golden, about 1 minute. To serve, cut into wedges. Yield: 4 portions.

Potato Omelet
(Frittata con le Patate)

4 tablespoons **Progresso Olive Oil**
1½ cups **cooked potatoes in ½-inch cubes**
½ cup **chopped onion**
6 **eggs**
2 tablespoons **water**
2 tablespoons **Progresso Grated Parmesan Cheese**
¼ teaspoon **salt**
⅛ teaspoon **ground black pepper**
2 tablespoons **finely chopped Progresso Tuscan Peppers**

Preheat broiler to hot. In a medium skillet heat olive oil until hot. Add potatoes. Sauté until pale gold. Add onion. Sauté onion and potatoes until potatoes are golden brown, adding more oil if necessary. In a medium bowl beat eggs, water, Parmesan cheese, salt and black pepper until blended. Spread potatoes evenly in skillet. Sprinkle with Tuscan peppers. Pour egg mixture over all. Cook over low heat until edge is set. With a spatula gently lift edge and tip skillet to allow uncooked egg to flow to the bottom. Cook until bottom is golden brown and top is almost set, about 10 minutes. Place skillet under broiler until top is golden. To serve, cut into wedges. Yield: 4 portions.

Quick Pepper Omelet
(Frittata di Peperoni)

1 jar (6 ounces) **Progresso Sweet Fried Peppers**
6 **eggs**
¼ teaspoon **salt**
1/16 teaspoon **ground black pepper**
2 tablespoons **butter**

Drain and chop sweet fried peppers, reserving about 1 teaspoon oil. In a medium bowl beat eggs, peppers, salt and black pepper until blended. In a medium skillet heat butter and reserved oil until hot. Add egg mixture. Cook over low heat until the edges set. With a spatula gently lift edge and tip skillet to allow uncooked egg to flow to the bottom. Cook until bottom is golden and top barely set. Carefully loosen omelet from bottom of pan with a spatula. Fold in half. Turn out onto a serving plate. Serve immediately. Yield: 4 portions.

Baked Artichoke Omelet
(Frittata al Forno con Carciofi)

6 eggs
2 tablespoons water
¾ teaspoon salt
½ teaspoon oregano leaves, crushed
⅛ teaspoon ground black pepper
⅛ teaspoon garlic powder
1 jar (6 ounces) Progresso Marinated Artichoke Hearts

Preheat oven to 350° F. In a medium bowl beat eggs, water, salt, oregano, black pepper and garlic powder until blended; set aside. Drain artichokes, reserving oil. Cut each artichoke into quarters. Measure 2 tablespoons of the reserved oil into a medium skillet with a heatproof handle. Add artichokes. Cook over low heat until hot, about 2 minutes, turning frequently. Remove skillet from heat. Pour in egg mixture. Place skillet in oven. Bake until omelet is set and very lightly browned, 15 to 17 minutes. Cut into quarters and serve at once. Yield: 4 portions.

Ham and Cheese Omelet Sicilian Style
(Frittata con Prosciutto e Formaggio alla Siciliana)

Adding bread crumbs makes this omelet foolproof.

2 tablespoons Progresso Olive Oil
1 tablespoon butter
1 cup green pepper strips
¾ cup chopped onion
7 eggs, lightly beaten
2 tablespoons water
¼ cup Progresso Grated Parmesan Cheese
¼ cup Progresso Italian-style Bread Crumbs
⅛ teaspoon ground black pepper
1 cup slivered ham

Preheat broiler to hot. In a medium skillet with a heatproof handle heat oil and butter until hot. Add green pepper and onion. Sauté until vegetables are tender, about 5 minutes; set aside. In a large bowl beat eggs, water, Parmesan cheese, bread crumbs and black pepper. Turn heat to medium low. Pour egg mixture over onions and green pepper. Cook until bottom is golden and top is almost set, about 10 minutes. Place skillet under broiler until top is golden, about 1 minute. To serve, cut in wedges. Yield: 4 portions.

Spaghetti Frittata
(Frittata di Spaghetti)
Sounds weird? Try it.

1½ cups hot cooked spaghetti (freshly cooked or reheated)
4 tablespoons butter, divided
3 eggs, lightly beaten
⅓ cup Progresso Grated Parmesan Cheese
2 tablespoons chopped fresh parsley
¼ teaspoon salt
⅛ teaspoon ground black pepper

Immediately after spaghetti has been cooked and drained, place in a medium bowl. Toss with 2 tablespoons of the butter. In a small bowl beat eggs, Parmesan cheese, parsley, salt and black pepper until blended. Pour over spaghetti. Toss to coat. In a medium skillet melt remaining 2 tablespoons butter. Add egg-spaghetti mixture. Cook over low heat until edge is set. With a spatula gently lift edge and tip skillet to allow uncooked egg to flow to the bottom. Cook until golden, about 2 minutes. Loosen edges with a spatula. Turn out onto a plate. Return to skillet, top side down. Cook until bottom is golden, about 2 minutes. To serve, cut into wedges. Yield: 3 portions.

Ham and Cheese Omelet Sicilian Style

Fettuccine Alfredo

1 cup heavy cream
6 tablespoons butter
1 package (12 ounces) fettuccine
1 cup Progresso Grated Parmesan Cheese
¼ teaspoon salt
¼ teaspoon ground black pepper
⅛ teaspoon ground nutmeg

In a saucepot large enough to hold all the cooked pasta place cream and butter. Cook over low heat until butter melts; set aside. Cook fettuccine according to package directions until just tender. Drain and transfer to the saucepot containing cream. Add Parmesan cheese, salt, black pepper and nutmeg. Cook over low heat, tossing gently, until fettuccine are evenly coated with sauce. Yield: 4 portions.

Pasta with Bacon Sauce
(Pasta all'Amatriciana)

*This marvelous bacon and tomato sauce is said to have originated in Amatrice,
a small town outside of Rome.*

8 slices bacon, diced
1 cup chopped onion
2 cloves garlic, minced
1 can (28 ounces) Progresso Crushed Tomatoes
½ cup Progresso Pepper Piccalilli
2½ teaspoons basil leaves, crushed
1¾ teaspoons salt, divided
¼ teaspoon ground black pepper
1 pound ground beef
1 package (16 ounces) spaghetti
3 tablespoons butter
½ cup Progresso Grated Parmesan Cheese

In a large skillet fry bacon until crisp. Drain on paper towels; set aside. Pour off all but 2 tablespoons of the bacon drippings from the skillet. Add onion and garlic. Sauté until tender, 3 to 4 minutes. Add tomatoes and liquid from pepper piccalilli. Chop peppers and add to the skillet along with basil, ¾ teaspoon of the salt and black pepper. Bring to a boil. Reduce heat and simmer, uncovered, until liquid is reduced and sauce is thickened, about 20 minutes, stirring often. Meanwhile, in a medium skillet sauté beef with remaining 1 teaspoon salt until brown. Cook spaghetti according to package directions just until tender. Drain; return to saucepot. Add butter and Parmesan cheese. Toss until butter melts. Cover to keep hot. Add reserved thickened sauce and meat. Cook for 5 minutes. To serve, place spaghetti on a large platter. Spoon on meat sauce. Sprinkle with crisp bacon.

Rotelle with Red Pepper Sauce
(Rotelle con Peperoni)

Sweet red peppers and hot red pepper flakes combine in this unusual sauce.

1 package (8 ounces) rotelle or other pasta
¼ cup Progresso Olive Oil
2 large cloves garlic
1 jar (7 ounces) Progresso Roasted Peppers
¼ teaspoon crushed red pepper (or to taste)
¼ teaspoon salt

Cook rotelle according to package directions until tender. Meanwhile, prepare sauce by heating olive oil in a medium saucepan until hot. Add garlic. Sauté until golden. Remove garlic and discard. Remove skillet from heat. Finely chop roasted peppers (or puree in a food processor). Add chopped peppers and crushed red pepper to skillet. Heat until hot. Drain rotelle and place in a serving bowl. Top with Red Pepper Sauce. Serve sprinkled with chopped parsley, if desired. Yield: 2 cups. Note: Recipe may be doubled.

Rotelle with Red Pepper Sauce
Pasta with Bacon Sauce

Baked Lasagne
(Lasagne al Forno)

2 tablespoons Progresso Olive Oil
1 cup chopped onion
2 cloves garlic, crushed
1½ pounds ground beef
2 cans (28 ounces each) Progresso Crushed Tomatoes
1 can (6 ounces) Progresso Tomato Paste
½ cup water
5 teaspoons oregano leaves, crushed
3 teaspoons salt, divided
¼ teaspoon ground black pepper, divided
3 eggs
2 containers (15 ounces each) ricotta cheese
1 package (16 ounces) lasagne
1 pound mozzarella cheese, sliced
6 tablespoons Progresso Grated Parmesan Cheese, divided

In a large skillet heat olive oil until hot. Add onion and garlic. Sauté until tender, about 5 minutes. Add beef. Cook and stir until brown, about 5 minutes. Pour off excess fat. Stir in crushed tomatoes, tomato paste, water, oregano, 2 teaspoons of the salt and ⅛ teaspoon of the black pepper. Bring to a boil. Reduce heat and simmer, uncovered, until thickened, 15 to 20 minutes, stirring frequently. Preheat oven to 350° F. In a medium bowl lightly beat eggs. Mix in ricotta cheese, remaining 1 teaspoon salt and ⅛ teaspoon black pepper. Cook lasagne according to package directions until just tender; drain. In a 13- x 9- x 2-inch baking pan spoon about one-quarter of the sauce (2 cups). Cover with one-third of the lasagne, one-half of the ricotta mixture and one-third of the mozzarella. Sprinkle with 2 tablespoons of the Parmesan cheese; repeat. Cover with a final layer of lasagne and a thin coating of the sauce. Cover and bake until hot and bubbly, about 1 hour. Uncover; top with remaining mozzarella and 2 tablespoons Parmesan cheese. Bake, uncovered, until cheese is melted, about 5 minutes. Remove from oven and let stand 10 minutes before serving. Serve with remaining sauce heated until hot. Yield: 10 portions.

Anchovy Clam Sauce
(Salsa di Vongole ed Acciughe)

4 tablespoons butter
2 tablespoons Progresso Olive Oil
3 tablespoons chopped fresh parsley
2 tablespoons minced onion
2 large cloves garlic, minced
½ teaspoon rosemary leaves, crushed
¼ teaspoon crushed red pepper
1 can (10½ ounces) Progresso White Clam Sauce
½ cup dry vermouth or white wine
4 anchovy fillets, finely chopped

In a large skillet heat butter and oil. Add parsley, onion, garlic, rosemary and crushed red pepper. Cook until garlic is light brown, about 1 minute. Drain clam sauce in a sieve, reserving clam liquid and clams separately. Add clam liquid and wine to skillet. Bring to a boil. Cook until liquid is reduced by half, about 3 minutes. Add anchovies and reserved clams. Heat until hot. Serve immediately over freshly cooked pasta. Yield: 1⅓ cups.

Spaghetti with Spinach and Clam Sauce
(Spaghetti con Spinaci e Vongole)

1 package (16 ounces) spaghetti
2 cans (10½ ounces each) Progresso White Clam Sauce
1 package (10 ounces) frozen chopped spinach, thawed
1½ teaspoons oregano leaves, crushed
⅛ teaspoon garlic powder
½ cup Progresso Grated Parmesan Cheese

Cook spaghetti according to package directions until just tender. Meanwhile, in a small saucepan combine clam sauce, spinach, oregano and garlic powder. Bring to a boil. Reduce heat and simmer, covered, for 5 minutes. Stir in Parmesan cheese. Drain spaghetti. Place in a serving bowl. Top with sauce. Toss gently. Serve with additional Parmesan cheese, if desired. Yield: 4 to 6 portions.

Pasta with Nut and Raisin Sauce
(Pasta alla Foriana)

Don't let the strange combination of ingredients stop you. It's a mouth-watering dish!

1 package (8 ounces) spaghetti
⅓ cup Progresso Olive Oil
¼ cup finely chopped walnuts
¼ cup finely chopped pignoli (pine nuts)
1 tablespoon minced garlic
1 teaspoon oregano leaves, crushed
⅓ cup golden raisins
2 tablespoons butter
½ teaspoon salt
¼ teaspoon ground black pepper
½ cup Progresso Grated Parmesan Cheese

Cook spaghetti according to package directions until just tender. Meanwhile, in a large skillet heat olive oil until hot. Add walnuts, pignoli, garlic and oregano. Cook until pignoli are light brown, about 3 minutes. Add raisins. Cook over low heat for 2 minutes. Drain spaghetti. Place in skillet with sauce. Add butter, salt and black pepper. Toss gently. Serve immediately with Parmesan cheese. Yield: 4 portions.

Fettuccine Fisherman's Style
(Fettuccine alla Pescatore)

2 tablespoons Progresso Olive Oil
1 cup chopped green peppers
1 tablespoon flour
2 cans (10½ ounces each) Progresso White Clam Sauce
¼ cup dry vermouth or white wine
½ teaspoon thyme leaves, crushed
¼ teaspoon oregano leaves, crushed
¼ teaspoon salt
⅛ teaspoon ground black pepper
12 ounces white fish fillets (cod, haddock or sole), cut in chunks
2 tablespoons Progresso Grated Parmesan Cheese
1 package (12 ounces) fettuccine

In a large saucepan heat olive oil until hot. Add green peppers. Sauté until barely tender. Sprinkle with flour; stir to blend. Add clam sauce, wine, thyme, oregano, salt and black pepper. Simmer, uncovered, for 10 minutes, stirring occasionally. Add fish. Simmer, uncovered, just until fish flakes easily when tested with a fork, about 2 minutes. Stir in Parmesan cheese. Cook fettuccine according to package directions until just tender. Drain. Place in a serving bowl. Add fish sauce. Toss gently. Yield: 4 portions (1 quart sauce).

Baked Ziti Parmigiano
(Ziti al Forno)

1 tablespoon Progresso Olive Oil
12 ounces ground beef
1 can (19 ounces) Progresso Minestrone Soup
1 can (8 ounces) Progresso Tomato Sauce
1½ teaspoons basil leaves, crushed
½ teaspoon oregano leaves, crushed
¼ teaspoon salt
⅛ teaspoon ground black pepper
1 package (8 ounces) ziti
½ cup Progresso Grated Parmesan Cheese, divided
4 ounces shredded mozzarella cheese

Preheat oven to 375° F. In a large saucepot heat olive oil until hot. Add beef. Cook and stir until meat is browned. Pour off excess fat. Add minestrone soup, tomato sauce, basil, oregano, salt and black pepper. Boil gently, uncovered, until slightly thickened and reduced to 3 cups, about 10 minutes, stirring occasionally. Meanwhile, cook ziti according to package directions until just tender. Drain. Spoon a thin layer of the meat mixture into a 9-inch square baking pan. Add the ziti. Top with remaining meat mixture. Sprinkle with half of the Parmesan cheese. Cover with mozzarella cheese and remaining Parmesan. Bake, uncovered, until cheese is golden brown, about 25 minutes. Yield: 4 portions.

Marinara Sauce
(Salsa Marinara)

1 tablespoon Progresso Olive Oil
½ cup chopped onion
1 garlic clove, crushed
1 can (28 ounces) Progresso Crushed Tomatoes
1 teaspoon salt
1 teaspoon Italian seasoning, crushed
1/16 teaspoon ground black pepper
2 tablespoons red wine

In a large saucepan heat olive oil until hot. Add onion and garlic. Sauté until tender, about 5 minutes. Add crushed tomatoes, salt, Italian seasoning and black pepper. Bring to a boil. Reduce heat and simmer, covered, for 10 minutes, stirring occasionally. Add wine. Simmer, covered, for 5 minutes. Serve over freshly cooked pasta, if desired. Yield: about 4 cups.

Vegetable Marinara
(Marinara del 'Estate)

2 tablespoons Progresso Olive Oil
1½ cups broccoli flowerets
1½ cups halved zucchini slices
1 can (10½ ounces) Progresso Chick Peas
1 jar (7 ounces) Progresso Roasted Peppers
1 jar (6 ounces) Progresso Marinated Mushrooms, undrained
¼ cup chopped fresh parsley
Marinara Sauce (recipe above)

In a large saucepan heat olive oil until hot. Add broccoli and zucchini. Cook and stir until crisp-tender, 3 to 5 minutes. Drain chick peas and dice roasted peppers. Stir into saucepan along with mushrooms and parsley. Add Marinara Sauce. Heat until hot. Serve over freshly cooked pasta and sprinkle with grated Parmesan cheese, if desired. Yield: about 5 cups.

Sausage Marinara
(Marinara al Salsiccie)

1 tablespoon Progresso Olive Oil
1 pound sweet Italian sausage links, cut in 1-inch lengths
Marinara Sauce (recipe above)
¼ teaspoon crushed red pepper

In a large saucepan heat olive oil until hot. Add sausage. Brown on all sides, about 5 minutes. Pour off drippings. Add Marinara Sauce and crushed red pepper. Heat until hot. Serve over freshly cooked pasta. Yield: about 5 cups.

Meatball Marinara
(Marinara con Polpette)

1 pound ground beef
½ cup Progresso Italian-style Bread Crumbs
¼ teaspoon salt
⅛ teaspoon ground black pepper
¾ cup water
1 egg, lightly beaten
Marinara Sauce (recipe above)

Preheat oven to 400° F. In a large bowl combine beef, bread crumbs, salt, black pepper, water and egg. Form into 1-inch balls (makes about 35). Place on an oiled jelly roll pan. Bake, uncovered, until browned, about 15 minutes. Add to Marinara Sauce. Heat until hot. Serve over freshly cooked pasta, if desired. Yield: about 5 cups.

Pesto

⅔ cup Progresso Olive Oil
2 large cloves garlic, coarsely chopped
½ teaspoon salt
¼ teaspoon ground black pepper
2 tablespoons pignoli (pine nuts) or chopped walnuts
2 cups loosely packed fresh basil leaves
½ cup loosely packed fresh parsley leaves
½ cup Progresso Grated Parmesan Cheese

In the container of an electric blender or food processor place olive oil, garlic, salt, black pepper, pignoli, basil and parsley. Cover and blend until smooth, scraping down the sides of the container as needed. Pour into a bowl. Stir in Parmesan cheese. Serve over pasta, vegetables, chicken or pizza. Yield: 1¼ cups.

Vegetable Marinara

Baked Semolina with Butter and Cheese
(Gnocchi alla Romana)

This is sometimes served with a simple light tomato sauce. A light, satisfying dish!

3 cups milk
3 cups water
1½ teaspoons salt
⅛ teaspoon ground nutmeg
1/16 teaspoon ground black pepper
1½ cups farina cereal (uncooked)
4 eggs
1¾ cups Progresso Grated Parmesan Cheese, divided
¼ cup butter, melted

Grease a 9-inch square baking pan; set aside. In a large saucepot combine milk, water, salt, nutmeg and black pepper. Bring to a boil. Over medium heat slowly add farina, stirring constantly with a wooden spoon, until mixture is very thick (the spoon will stand unsupported in the middle of the pot). Remove from heat. Beat eggs and 1½ cups of the Parmesan cheese until blended. Gradually add to hot farina, stirring constantly. Spoon into prepared baking pan, smoothing the top with a metal spatula dipped in hot water. Cover and refrigerate until firm, about 1 hour. Preheat oven to 400° F. Uncover pan and pour melted butter over the top. Sprinkle with remaining ¼ cup Parmesan cheese. Bake until firm and light brown, about 30 minutes. Remove from oven. Cut into 3- x 1½-inch rectangles. Serve hot instead of potatoes, pasta or rice. (Cover and refrigerate any remaining gnocchi. To reheat, bake, covered, in a preheated 350° F oven until hot, about 15 minutes.) Yield: 8 to 12 portions.

Spaghetti Carbonara
(Spaghetti alla Carbonara)

Actually spaghetti with bacon and eggs.

8 ounces sliced bacon, chopped
⅓ cup dry vermouth or white wine
3 eggs
¾ cup Progresso Grated Parmesan Cheese
⅓ cup chopped fresh parsley
½ teaspoon ground black pepper
½ teaspoon salt
1 package (16 ounces) spaghetti

In a large skillet fry bacon until crisp. Drain on paper towels; set aside. Pour off all but 1 tablespoon of the bacon drippings from the skillet. Add wine. Cook and stir over low heat, scraping brown particles from bottom of skillet. Cook until wine has almost evaporated; set aside. In a bowl large enough to hold the cooked pasta combine eggs, Parmesan cheese, parsley, black pepper and salt. Cook spaghetti according to package directions until just tender. Drain. Transfer to the bowl containing the egg mixture. Add reserved bacon and wine mixture. Toss until spaghetti is well coated. Yield: 4 to 6 portions.

Noodles with Walnut Sauce
(Tagliatelle al Noci)

4 tablespoons butter
½ cup chopped walnuts
3 tablespoons Progresso Italian-style Bread Crumbs
1 package (8 ounces) broad noodles
½ cup heavy cream, heated
¼ teaspoon salt
⅛ teaspoon ground black pepper

In a large skillet melt butter. Add walnuts. Sauté until butter is lightly browned and nuts are lightly toasted. Remove from heat. Sprinkle with bread crumbs; mix gently. Cook noodles according to package directions until just tender. Drain and transfer to a large bowl. Add crumb mixture, cream, salt and black pepper; toss gently. Yield: 4 portions.

Pizza with Peppers and Sausage, page 58

Calzone

This is pizza dough cut in rounds and filled to make turnovers.

1 pound Pizza Dough (see page 56)
4 ounces thinly sliced Italian salami
8 ounces sliced mozzarella cheese
  Onion powder
  Garlic powder
  Oregano leaves, crushed
  Ground black pepper
  Progresso Olive Oil
  Milk

Place rack as low in oven as possible. Preheat oven to 350° F. On a lightly floured surface, roll pizza dough ⅛ inch thick. Cut into 4-inch circles. Cut Italian salami and mozzarella cheese into ½-inch-wide strips. Place a few pieces of salami on one side of each round. Top with a few strips of cheese. Sprinkle each round with ⅛ teaspoon onion powder and ¹⁄₁₆ teaspoon each garlic powder and oregano, a dash of black pepper and a few drops of olive oil. Fold dough over the filling. Press edges firmly together. Place on a greased baking sheet. Brush tops with milk. Bake until golden, 25 to 30 minutes. Yield: 20.

Easy to Make Pan Pizza
(Pizza Facile)

About 40 minutes from start to finish.

1 pound sweet Italian sausage links
½ cup chopped onion
1 can (14¾ ounces) Progresso Pizza Sauce or
  1 jar (15½ ounces) Progresso Marinara
  Spaghetti Sauce
1 cup shredded mozzarella cheese
2 eggs
1 cup milk
1 tablespoon Progresso Olive Oil
1 cup unsifted all-purpose flour
½ teaspoon salt
6 tablespoons Progresso Grated Parmesan
  Cheese, divided
¼ teaspoon oregano leaves, crushed

Preheat oven to 400° F. Cut sausage into ½-inch slices. In a large skillet fry sausage until browned on all sides, about 5 minutes. With a slotted spoon remove sausage. Pour off all but 2 tablespoons of the drippings. Add onion. Cook and stir until tender, about 5 minutes. Return sausage to skillet. Stir in pizza sauce. Bring to a boil. Reduce heat and simmer, uncovered, for 5 minutes. Pour mixture into an ungreased 13- x 9- x 2-inch baking pan. Sprinkle with mozzarella cheese. In a medium bowl beat eggs, milk and olive oil until blended. Add flour, salt and 2 tablespoons of the Parmesan cheese. Beat until smooth. Pour batter over cheese in pan. Sprinkle with oregano and remaining 4 tablespoons Parmesan cheese. Bake until crust is golden, 20 to 25 minutes. Serve at once. Yield: 6 portions.

Individual Pepper Pizzas
(Pizzete Vivace)

1 jar (3¾ ounces) Progresso Marinated
  Mushrooms
1 package (8 ounces) refrigerator crescent
  dinner rolls
¾ cup drained Progresso Pepper Piccalilli

Preheat oven to 375° F. Lightly grease a cookie sheet. Drain and halve marinated mushrooms; set aside. Place each crescent roll flat on the prepared cookie sheet. Top each with equal amounts of pepper piccalilli and mushrooms. Bake until pastry is golden brown, 10 to 15 minutes. Cut in halves, if desired. Yield: 8 to 16 wedges.

New Way Pizza
(Pizza al Uso Nuovo)
A quickly mixed batter forms the crust.

1½ pounds ground beef
1 can (14¾ ounces) Progresso Pizza Sauce or
   1 jar (15½ ounces) Progresso Marinara
   Spaghetti Sauce
2 teaspoons salt, divided
1 teaspoon onion powder
¼ teaspoon garlic powder
1 cup unsifted all-purpose flour
⅔ cup milk
2 eggs
1 jar (6 ounces) Progresso Sweet Fried
   Peppers, drained
4 ounces sliced mozzarella cheese

Place rack as low as possible in the oven. Preheat oven to 425° F. Lightly grease and flour a 15- x 10- x 1-inch jelly roll pan; set aside. In a large skillet cook and stir beef until browned, about 5 minutes; pour off drippings. Stir in about one-third of the pizza sauce, 1½ teaspoons of the salt, onion powder and garlic powder. Simmer, uncovered, for 1 minute; set aside. In a small bowl combine flour, milk, eggs and the remaining ½ teaspoon salt; mix until smooth. Pour batter into prepared pan, tilting pan so batter covers the bottom evenly. Spoon meat mixture evenly over the top. Bake for 25 minutes. Remove from oven. Drizzle with remaining pizza sauce. Arrange peppers and mozzarella cheese on top. Return to oven until cheese is melted, about 5 minutes. Yield: 6 to 8 portions.

Italian Bread Crisps
(Pane con Olio e Briciole)
A tasty way to serve Italian bread.

3 tablespoons Progresso Olive Oil
3 tablespoons Progresso Italian-style Bread
   Crumbs
1 Italian Bread (about 14 ounces)

Preheat oven to 400° F. In a small bowl combine olive oil and bread crumbs. Cut Italian bread in half lengthwise. Spread cut surfaces with crumb mixture. Place bread on a baking pan. Bake, uncovered, until hot and crispy, about 6 minutes. Cut into slices and serve hot. Yield: about 16 slices.

Spinach and Ricotta Torte
(Torta di Ricotta e Spinaci)
An easy-to-serve, nourishing main dish for vegetarians and non-vegetarians alike.

½ recipe Pizza Dough (page 56) or
   1 pound frozen pizza or bread dough
1 package (10 ounces) frozen chopped
   spinach, thawed
4 eggs
1 container (15 ounces) ricotta cheese
⅓ cup Progresso Grated Parmesan Cheese
½ teaspoon basil leaves, crushed
½ teaspoon salt
⅛ teaspoon ground black pepper
⅛ teaspoon ground nutmeg
1 jar (7 ounces) Progresso Roasted Peppers

Place rack as low as possible in the oven. Preheat oven to 425° F. Grease a 9-inch layer cake pan with a removable bottom. On a lightly floured surface roll out dough to a 13-inch circle. Fit dough into prepared pan and crimp edge. Squeeze out as much liquid as possible from the spinach. In a large mixing bowl beat together eggs, ricotta and Parmesan cheeses, spinach, basil, salt, black pepper and nutmeg. Chop roasted peppers. Stir into cheese mixture. Turn into prepared crust. Bake for 15 minutes. Lower oven temperature to 375° F. Bake until crust is browned and a knife inserted in the center comes out clean, 30 to 45 minutes. Remove rim from pan. Cool on a rack for 10 minutes. Yield: 6 to 8 portions.

Crustless Pizza
(Pizza Nuda)

1 jar (7 ounces) Progresso Roasted Peppers
5 ounces sweet Italian sausage links
6 eggs
2 tablespoons milk
1 teaspoon oregano leaves, crushed
½ teaspoon salt
¼ teaspoon ground black pepper
2 tablespoons Progresso Olive Oil
1 can (8 ounces) Progresso Tomato Sauce
½ cup shredded mozzarella cheese

Preheat broiler to hot. Cut roasted peppers into bite-sized pieces; set aside. Cut sausage into ½-inch slices. In a 10-inch skillet with a heatproof handle fry sausage until brown on all sides, about 5 minutes. With a slotted spoon remove sausage. Pour off all but 1 tablespoon of the drippings. In a large bowl beat eggs, milk, oregano, salt and black pepper. Add olive oil to skillet; heat until hot. Add egg mixture. Cook over low heat until the edges set. With a spatula gently lift edges and tip skillet to allow uncooked egg to flow to the bottom. When egg mixture is brown on the bottom and firm on the top, remove skillet from heat. Spoon ½ cup of the tomato sauce over the top. Sprinkle with mozzarella cheese. Top with peppers and sausages. Place under broiler 3 to 4 inches from heat source until cheese is melted and mixture bubbles, 2 to 3 minutes. Set pan on a wire rack for a minute to set. Cut into wedges. Heat remaining tomato sauce; serve with pizza. Yield: 4 to 6 portions.

Pizza Dough

1 package active dry yeast
1⅓ cups warm water (105-115° F)
2 teaspoons salt
2 tablespoons Progresso Olive Oil
4 cups unsifted all-purpose flour
   (approximate)

In a large mixing bowl dissolve yeast in warm water. Add salt, olive oil and 1½ cups of the flour. With an electric beater set at medium, beat until blended. Reduce speed to low. Beat in remaining flour, about ½ cup at a time, until mixture comes together to form a soft dough which can be kneaded. (Dough can also be beaten with a wooden spoon.) Turn dough onto a lightly floured board. Knead until smooth and elastic. Place dough in an oiled bowl. Turn dough to oil entire surface. Cover and let rise in a warm place until double in bulk, 1 to 1½ hours. Punch dough down and divide in half. Use immediately or wrap in plastic wrap and refrigerate overnight or freeze. Bring to room temperature before using. Yield: two 12- to 14-inch pizza crusts (about 2 pounds dough).
Note: recipe may be halved; use 1¼ teaspoons yeast.

Italian Sausage and Peppers
(Salsiccie e Peperoni)

1 pound Italian sweet sausage links
2 cups green pepper strips
2 cups coarsely chopped onions
1 jar (7 ounces) Progresso Roasted Peppers
2 cans (8 ounces each) Progresso Tomato
   Sauce
8 Italian hard rolls

Pierce sausage with fork tines. Heat a large skillet until hot. Add sausages. Cook until browned. Add green peppers and onions. Cook until peppers are tender and onions are transparent. Cut roasted peppers into strips. Add to skillet along with tomato sauce. Simmer, covered, for 20 minutes. Split rolls in half lengthwise, without cutting through completely. Fill with sausage mixture. Serve hot. Yield: 8 portions.

Country Style Pizza
(Pizza Rustica)

1 package (13¾ ounces) hot roll mix
2 eggs, lightly beaten
2 containers (15 ounces each) ricotta cheese
½ cup Progresso Grated Parmesan Cheese
½ cup chopped Progresso Roasted Peppers
⅛ teaspoon ground black pepper
4 ounces sliced prosciutto ham, slivered

Place rack as low as possible in the oven. Preheat oven to 425° F. Prepare hot roll mix as package label directs for making pizza crust. Cover lightly. Let dough rest for 5 minutes. Divide dough in half. Pat half of the dough into the bottom of an oiled 12- x 8- x 2-inch baking pan, stretching dough to the edges. Cover lightly. Place pan over a skillet containing boiling water until dough rises about ¼ inch, 2 to 3 minutes. Combine eggs, ricotta and Parmesan cheeses, roasted peppers and black pepper. Spread over dough to within ½ inch of the edge. Top with prosciutto. On a floured board roll out remaining dough to fit on top of ricotta mixture. Press edges of dough together to seal. Bake until brown, about 40 minutes. Yield: 6 portions.

Salami and Spinach Pie
(Pasticcio di Salami e Spinaci)

1 package (10 ounces) frozen chopped spinach, thawed
2 tablespoons Progresso Olive Oil
2 cups thinly sliced mushrooms
4 eggs
1 container (15 ounces) ricotta cheese
¾ cup shredded fontina cheese
½ teaspoon oregano leaves, crushed
½ teaspoon salt
⅛ teaspoon ground black pepper
1 jar (6 ounces) Progresso Sweet Fried Peppers
9-inch baked pie shell with high rim, chilled or 9-inch frozen deep dish pie shell, thawed
3 ounces thinly-sliced Italian salami, slivered

Place rack in the lower third of the oven. Preheat oven to 425° F. Squeeze as much liquid from the spinach as possible; set aside. In a medium skillet heat olive oil until hot. Add mushrooms. Sauté until light brown; set aside. In a large mixing bowl beat eggs, ricotta and fontina cheeses, oregano, salt, black pepper and reserved spinach until blended. Stir in sweet fried peppers and reserved mushrooms. Pour into pie shell. Arrange salami in a decorative pattern on the top. Bake for 15 minutes. Lower temperature to 375° F. Bake until a knife inserted in the center comes out clean, 35 to 45 minutes. Cool for 10 minutes before serving. Yield: 6 portions.

Pizza Loaf
(Pane Ripiene)

1 Italian bread (about 9 ounces)
1 jar (9¾ ounces) Progresso Olive Salad (Olive Condite)
1 jar (7 ounces) Progresso Roasted Peppers
¾ cup Progresso Pizza or Marinara Spaghetti Sauce
2 ounces very thinly sliced Italian salami
½ cup shredded mozzarella cheese
¼ cup Progresso Grated Parmesan Cheese

Preheat oven to 350° F. Slice off the top quarter of the bread; remove the inside leaving a shell about ½ inch thick. Place loaf on a baking sheet. Drain the liquid from olive salad, reserving 3 tablespoons of the liquid. Use liquid to brush the inside and top edge of loaf. Thinly slice roasted peppers. Spoon pizza sauce, olive salad and roasted peppers into loaf. Tuck salami slices around the edge, pressing down gently to form a rim. Sprinkle mozzarella and Parmesan cheeses over the top. Bake, uncovered, until filling is hot and cheese melts, about 30 minutes. Cut in thick slices with a serrated knife. Yield: 4 to 6 portions.

Italian Pepper and Crackling Bread
(Tortano)

A delectable bread which goes well with sliced tomatoes and ham.
The amount of black pepper is correct.

1 pound salt pork
5½ cups all-purpose flour (unsifted)
2 packages active dry yeast
2 tablespoons sugar
4 teaspoons basil leaves, crushed
2 teaspoons salt
1½ teaspoons ground black pepper
1½ cups warm water (120-130° F)

Remove and discard rind from salt pork; cut into ½-inch cubes. In a medium skillet over moderate heat cook salt pork until browned and crisp. Remove cracklings (pork bits) from fat; set aside. Reserve 3 tablespoons fat for later use. In the large bowl of an electric mixer combine 3 cups of the flour, yeast, sugar, basil, salt and black pepper: Gradually add water and 2 tablespoons of the reserved fat, mixing at low speed until blended. Mix at high speed for 3 minutes. With a wooden spoon stir in pork bits and enough flour to make a stiff dough (about 1 cup). Turn dough onto a lightly floured board. Knead in enough flour to make a stiff dough (1 to 1½ cups). Place in a lightly greased bowl. Turn dough to grease entire surface. Cover lightly. Let rise in a warm place until doubled in bulk, about 45 minutes. Punch down dough. Cut into three equal pieces. On a lightly floured board roll each piece into a 10- x 12-inch rectangle. Roll up jelly-roll fashion. Shape into a circle; dampen ends with water and pinch together to fasten. Place on greased baking sheets. Brush lightly with remaining 1 tablespoon fat. Cover lightly. Let rise in a warm place until doubled in bulk, about 30 minutes. Place rack as low as possible in the oven. Preheat oven to 375° F. Bake until breads sound hollow when lightly tapped, about 30 minutes. Cool on wire racks. Yield: three 12-ounce loaves.

Pizza with Peppers and Sausage
(Pizza Peperonata con Salsiccie)

Everything you ever wanted in a pizza.

1 recipe Pizza Dough (page 56)
1 can (28 ounces) Progresso Crushed Tomatoes
1 tablespoon Progresso Wine Vinegar
1 teaspoon salt
1 teaspoon Italian seasoning
½ teaspoon sugar
⅛ teaspoon ground black pepper
½ cup Progresso Grated Parmesan Cheese
2 jars (6 ounces each) Progresso Sweet Fried Peppers
4 ounces sliced pepperoni sausage
12 ounces shredded mozzarella cheese

Let pizza dough rise according to recipe directions. Meanwhile, in a large saucepan combine crushed tomatoes, wine vinegar, salt, Italian seasoning, sugar and black pepper. Bring to a boil. Reduce heat and simmer, uncovered, until slightly thickened, about 10 minutes. Cool to room temperature. Place rack as low as possible in the oven. Preheat oven to 425° F. Punch down dough. Fit into two oiled 12-inch pizza pans, stretching dough over the edge to allow for shrinkage. Spread one-half of the tomato mixture over each pizza. Sprinkle with Parmesan cheese. Arrange sweet fried peppers and pepperoni sausage on top. Sprinkle with mozzarella cheese. Bake one at a time until crust is golden and cheese is melted, 15 to 20 minutes. Yield: two 12-inch pizzas.

DESSERTS

Biscuit Tortoni
(Gelatina di Crema)

2 eggs, separated
⅓ cup confectioners sugar
½ cup plus 1 tablespoon crushed Italian dry
   macaroons (about 3½ ounces)
2 tablespoons dark rum
2 teaspoons pure vanilla extract
1 cup heavy cream, whipped
   Maraschino cherries

In a large bowl beat egg yolks and sugar until mixture is pale yellow. Stir in ½ cup of the Italian macaroons, rum and vanilla extract. In a medium bowl beat egg whites until stiff peaks form. Fold egg whites and whipped cream into macaroon mixture. Spoon into paper cupcake pan liners. Sprinkle with remaining 1 tablespoon crushed macaroons. Garnish each with a cherry and freeze until firm. Yield: 8 to 10 portions.

Zabaglione

6 egg yolks
⅓ cup sugar
¾ cup sweet Marsala wine
1 strip lemon peel (yellow portion only)
1 cup heavy cream, whipped

In the top of a double boiler over hot water beat egg yolks, sugar, Marsala and lemon peel until mixture thickens, about 20 minutes. Remove from heat. Cool to room temperature. Discard lemon peel. Fold in whipped cream. Pour into dessert glasses. Garnish with chopped walnuts, if desired. Yield: 4 to 6 portions.

Ricotta Cheesecake
(Crostata di Ricotta)

1 cup unsifted all-purpose flour
1 tablespoon sugar
¼ teaspoon salt
¼ cup butter
1 egg yolk
1½ tablespoons ice water
2 containers (15 ounces each) ricotta cheese
4 eggs
1 cup sugar
2 tablespoons cornstarch
4 teaspoons grated lemon peel
3 tablespoons lemon juice
1 teaspoon pure vanilla extract
1 cup heavy cream

Preheat oven to 400° F. In a medium bowl combine flour, sugar and salt. Cut in butter until mixture resembles coarse crumbs. With a fork stir egg yolk and water into crumb mixture. With hands gently shape pastry into a ball. On a lightly floured surface roll out pastry ⅛ inch thick. Fit into bottom and part way up the sides of a 9-inch springform pan. Prick bottom all over with fork tines. Refrigerate for 10 minutes. Bake until pale gold, about 8 minutes. Cool. In the container of an electric blender or food processor place half of the ricotta cheese; add the eggs, sugar, cornstarch, lemon peel, lemon juice and vanilla extract. Cover and blend until smooth. Turn into a large bowl. Blend remaining ricotta cheese with heavy cream until smooth. Stir into cheese and egg mixture. Pour into pastry-lined pan. Reduce oven temperature to 350° F. Bake until golden and firm to the touch, about 1¼ hours. Turn off oven, leaving cake in oven for 2 hours. Cool completely in pan. Yield: 10 to 12 portions.

Honey Balls
(Struffoli)

2 cups water
1 cup butter
¼ teaspoon salt
3½ cups unsifted all-purpose flour
6 eggs
1⅓ cups honey
1 container (4 ounces) diced candied orange
  peel
1 container (4 ounces) candied cherries
2 tablespoons grated lemon peel

Preheat oven to 350° F. In a large saucepan bring water, butter and salt to a rolling boil. Boil until butter is melted. Stir in flour all at once. Reduce heat and beat well for 1 minute. Remove from heat. Beat in eggs one at a time, beating well after each addition, until mixture is smooth and shiny. Drop mixture by ½ teaspoonfuls onto greased cookie sheets, 1 inch apart. Bake until golden, about 20 minutes. Cool on wire racks. In a large saucepan bring honey, orange peel, cherries and lemon peel to a boil. Boil for 2 minutes; remove from heat. Add puffs, a few at a time, tossing well to coat. Remove with a slotted spoon to a serving plate. Repeat until all puffs are coated. With wet hands, stack puffs in a pyramid. Yield: 10 to 12 portions (8 dozen).

Christmas Fruitcake Candy
(Panforte di Siena)

1½ cups coarsely chopped walnuts or
  hazelnuts
1 cup coarsely chopped almonds
1 cup chopped dried figs or golden raisins
1 container (4 ounces) diced candied orange
  peel
1 container (4 ounces) diced candied lemon
  peel
1 container (4 ounces) diced candied citron
1 container (4 ounces) diced candied
  pineapple
½ cup unsweetened cocoa
⅓ cup all-purpose flour (unsifted)
2 teaspoons ground cinnamon
1 teaspoon ground cloves
¾ cup honey
¾ cup sugar

Preheat oven to 300° F. Grease and flour a 9-inch springform pan; set aside. In a large bowl mix walnuts, almonds, figs, orange peel, lemon peel, citron, pineapple, cocoa, flour, cinnamon and cloves. In a medium saucepan combine honey and sugar. Bring to a boil, stirring constantly. Reduce heat and simmer, uncovered, until a little of the syrup dropped into cold water forms a soft ball, about 4 minutes. Do not overcook. Pour syrup over nut-fruit mixture, tossing well. Press into prepared pan, smoothing top. Bake until firm, about 40 minutes. Cool in pan. Remove sides of pan. Sprinkle with confectioners sugar, if desired. Serve in thin wedges as a confection. Yield: about 20 wedges.

Pine Nut Cookies
(Biscotti di Pignoli)

These delicate, crispy cookies go well with fruit ices, mixed fruits or Zabaglione.

3 eggs (at room temperature)
1 cup sugar
1⅓ cups unsifted all-purpose flour
⅛ teaspoon salt
½ teaspoon pure vanilla extract
½ cup pignoli (pine nuts)

Preheat oven to 375° F. In a large bowl of an electric mixer beat eggs and sugar until light and lemon-colored and mixture leaves a thick trail when beaters are lifted, 4 to 5 minutes. Stir in flour, salt and vanilla extract. Drop by teaspoonfuls 1 inch apart onto greased cookie sheets. Place a few pignoli nuts on top of each cookie. Let stand for 5 minutes. Bake until edges are golden, about 10 minutes. Cool on wire racks. Yield: about 5 dozen.

Cassata Siciliana, page 63
Stuffed Peaches, page 63
Pine Nut Cookies

Cassata Siciliana

The Queen of Desserts.

1 container (15 ounces) ricotta cheese
⅓ cup sugar
3 tablespoons dark rum
2 ounces semi-sweet chocolate, coarsely grated
½ cup diced mixed candied fruit
¼ cup heavy cream, whipped
1 frozen pound cake (10¾ ounces), cut in ½-inch slices
Chocolate Frosting (recipe follows)

In a large mixing bowl beat together ricotta cheese, sugar, dark rum and semi-sweet chocolate until evenly blended. Stir in candied fruit. Fold in whipped cream. Butter a 2-quart bowl. Line bottom and sides with pound cake slices, cutting slices as necessary to fit. Spoon about half the cream mixture into the bowl. Cover with a layer of cake slices and remaining cream mixture. Arrange remaining cake slices on top. If any side cake pieces come above filling, cut them off and arrange attractively on top of Cassata. Cover with plastic wrap and refrigerate overnight. To unmold, loosen sides of Cassata with a flexible metal spatula. Turn Cassata upside down on a serving platter. Dip a kitchen towel into boiling water. Carefully wring out water. Wrap towel around Cassata. Repeat dipping the towel in boiling water, wringing out water and wrapping the Cassata with the towel until Cassata drops from the bowl. Frost top and sides with Chocolate Frosting. Garnish with glazed cherries, if desired. To serve, cut in wedges. Yield: about 10 portions.

Chocolate Frosting

5 ounces semi-sweet chocolate
¼ cup brewed coffee
1 egg
2 cups sifted confectioners sugar
½ cup butter (at room temperature)
1 teaspoon pure vanilla extract

In the top of a double boiler over simmering water cook chocolate and coffee until chocolate melts. Remove from heat. Beat in egg. Transfer to a large mixing bowl. Gradually beat in sugar. Add butter, about 1 tablespoon at a time, and vanilla extract, beating until frosting is smooth and creamy and of good spreading consistency. Yield: about 2½ cups.

Stuffed Peaches
(Pesche Ripiene)

This is one of the most luscious of summer desserts made with fresh peaches.

4 ripe peaches (about 1½ pounds)
1 cup dry Marsala
¼ cup water
⅓ cup sugar
1 cup crushed Italian dry macaroons (about 7 ounces)
½ cup heavy cream, whipped
1 teaspoon pure vanilla extract

Cut peaches in halves; remove pits. Scoop out part of the peach pulp and chop (makes about ½ cup); set aside. In a small saucepan bring Marsala, water and sugar to a boil. Add 4 peach halves at a time, spooning some of the liquid over the peaches. Reduce heat and simmer, covered, for 5 minutes. Remove peach halves; set aside. Repeat with remaining peach halves. Remove skins, if desired; cool. Mix reserved peach pulp with Italian macaroons, whipped cream and vanilla extract. Place peaches in a serving dish cavity side up. Spoon peach-cream mixture into cavities. Pour syrup around peaches. Cover and refrigerate until chilled. Garnish with additional crushed macaroons, if desired. Yield: 8 stuffed peach halves.

INDEX